Multimedia Learning Stations

**Recent Titles in the Libraries Unlimited
Tech Tools for Learning Series**

The Networked Library: A Guide for the Educational Use of Social Networking Sites
Melissa A. Purcell

Bookmarking: Beyond the Basics
Alicia E. Vandenbroek

School Library Infographics: How to Create Them, Why to Use Them
Peggy Milam Creighton

3D Printing: A Powerful New Curriculum Tool for Your School Library
Lesley M. Cano

Multimedia Learning Stations

Facilitating Instruction, Strengthening the Research Process, Building Collaborative Partnerships

JEN SPISAK

Foreword by Ann M. Martin

TECH TOOLS FOR LEARNING
JUDI REPMAN, SERIES EDITOR

 LIBRARIES
UNLIMITED™

An Imprint of ABC-CLIO, LLC

Santa Barbara, California • Denver, Colorado

Library of Congress Cataloging-in-Publication Data

Spisak, Jen.
    Multimedia learning stations : facilitating instruction, strengthening the research process, building collaborative partnerships / Jen Spisak.
        pages cm.—(Tech tools for learning)
    Includes bibliographical references and index.
    ISBN 978-1-4408-3517-9 (paperback) — ISBN 978-1-4408-3518-6
(ebook)   1. Interactive multimedia.   2. Classroom learning
centers.   3. Computer-assisted instruction.   4. Media programs
(Education)   I. Title.
    LB1028.55.S75 2015
    371.33—dc23   2015017304
ISBN: 978-1-4408-3517-9
EISBN: 978-1-4408-3518-6

19 18 17 16 15   1 2 3 4 5

This book is also available on the World Wide Web as an eBook.
Visit www.abc-clio.com for details.

Libraries Unlimited
An Imprint of ABC-CLIO, LLC

ABC-CLIO, LLC
130 Cremona Drive, P.O. Box 1911
Santa Barbara, California 93116-1911

This book is printed on acid-free paper ∞

Manufactured in the United States of America

For Jamie, Paige, and Lila Spisak

Contents

Foreword

Generating the same steadfast loyalty for a library program that fans display at a sporting event is extremely important in today's educational climate. That is why *Multimedia Learning Stations: Facilitating Instruction, Strengthening the Research Process, Building Collaborative Partnerships* is essential reading for anyone seeking to create excitement and enthusiasm for their library program.

In this book, readers witness firsthand how a library program went from a place that was mildly embraced to a position where the educational community is unwavering in its need and desire to integrate library experiences into student learning. Aligned to the American Association of School Librarians' (AASL's) learning standards and program guidelines, this book is the ultimate handbook for transforming learning in the library.

Jen Spisak is exceptionally well-suited to guide us through the process of moving to a stations-based approach to learning. Her experiences, published articles, presentations, and awards demonstrate the depth of her understanding of the secondary library environment. Each lesson she creates focuses on addressing students' multiple intelligences and varied learning styles. Hungary Creek Middle School in Henrico County, Virginia, where she is librarian, is a model for multimedia learning stations. She is an accomplished librarian, and was named Virginia's 2012 School Librarian of the Year.

Collaboration is essential to Jen's program. She partners with every curriculum department, knows the curriculum standards for each content area, and integrates subject area standards with library learning standards at a pace that brings hundreds of students into her library daily.

As a single librarian in a middle school of just under 900 diverse students, Jen instructs continuously. What make the lessons successful are the joint preplanning, the co-teaching, and the final assessment of the lessons. Jen believes in continuous improvement, and knows that evaluation of the plan, activities, and resources utilized will improve instruction. There is no one better qualified to help us understand how to construct engaging learning experiences than Jen Spisak.

This book covers it all, including how to attract teachers into the library, what multimedia learning stations are, why stations should be used, what types of stations can be created, when to use stations, how to assess student learning, and much more. The level of detail in this book will benefit the reader as they use the information to create and organize an activity- and standards-based station approach to learning.

Knowing what works and what does not work is especially useful. Each chapter provides the reader with strategies for success in implementing 21st-century and information literacy skills. Each chapter provides tips on how students can enhance their learning of content standards through self-guided practice. The "Try Three Before You Ask Me" policy is an example of training students to be accountable for their research.

A strong point of this publication is its real-life examples. Included are pictures, charts, lists, and process steps, to enable the reader to move into a stations approach to student instruction. Each chapter is packed with information, ideas, and useful processes to guide the reader.

One of the most useful chapters covers how to move students from station to station.

As students take responsibility for their learning, it is important to transition them to a facilitative environment. Explained clearly is how to draw from the teacher's knowledge of their students to decide on the best method of moving students from station to station.

Discover how using rotation time wisely creates opportunities to connect students to the curriculum topic they are researching. Don't miss the chapter on steps to take when creating multimedia learning stations. This chapter contains information that guides the reader on how to calculate the length of time for each station. The book even walks the reader thought organizing and implementing the stations. These chapters deliver basic ideas and techniques for station rotation, creating stations, and implementing an engaging, effective learning experience.

The chapters on questioning and assessment are strong and self-contained enough to stand alone. They can be used in any lesson with any topic. When using the information from these two chapters, users of this book will discover how to create quality questions in four steps and incorporate assessment into stations. An incredibly important aspect of these chapters is how to loop the teacher into the process. It is clear that this partnership makes for a richer and more successful lesson.

In the chapter on questioning, the author provides four steps to use when creating quality questions. She describes which of the steps can be worked on collaboratively with teachers. Bloom's Taxonomy, and Lorin W. Anderson and David R. Krathwohl's new version of Bloom, are explained in the context of developing multimedia stations that stimulate student thinking. Constructing higher level questions at each station, even when data, dates, and facts are required, shows students that it is important to think about the information they have researched. Examples of some of Jen's lessons include clearly marked Thinking Questions. These well-developed questions encourage students to synthesize and analyze information.

Assessment is another topic covered in this book that can be used by the reader to strengthen any lesson. The topic of assessment is rich with definitions, examples, and strategies for creating student self-assessment methods that work. It includes examples of assessment tools, both digital and print. In the current educational environment, librarians must show that they contribute to academic achievement. The assessment chapter provides librarians with tools that measure individual student growth. The suggestions provide strategies to measure how well students master the indicators in AASL's *Standards for the 21st-Century Learner*. Also, the assessment chapter indicates how the reader can use data to improve lessons and garner support for the library program.

Rather than leave the reader on their own to create stations, Jen Spisak finishes the book off with actual samples of multimedia learning stations. This gives the reader an opportunity to get started immediately. These lessons span the secondary level, middle through high school. Each multimedia learning station lesson includes curriculum content standards, AASL's *Standards for the 21st-Century Learner*, actual stations including questions, and a resource list. By selecting one of these lessons and adapting it for your students, you will see for yourself a powerful transformation in staff participation and student learning.

The satisfying outcome for users of this book is that students and staff *will* be drawn into the library like fans to a sporting event. Once in the library, students will become skilled, responsible users of information and self-evaluators of their learning. It is a win-win for the library program, staff, and students.

Ann M. Martin

Acknowledgments

Writing a book is hard. Really hard. It takes time, energy, dedication, and many sleepless nights. It is definitely a task I could not have completed on my own, and I am terribly grateful for all of the souls who helped me make this book a reality:

Joe Recchi, Laura McCutcheon, Shannon Hyman, Charmaine Monds, and Susan Loan, who helped me edit and revise various chapters of this book throughout my writing process, and Nancy Essid, who developed a presentation with me on student self-assessment that provided much of the research for the chapter on assessment. All of their comments, suggestions, help, and edits were invaluable.

The staff members at Hungary Creek Middle School, who collaborate with me on a daily basis, and trust me with their students and their content. They have taught me so much about what it means to be a good educator and a great friend.

My principal, Robbi Moose, whose support of our library program and of me is unwavering.

The students at Hungary Creek, who inspire me daily and offer kind suggestions for improvement.

My mentor and friend Heather Brandenburg, who shared that first set of learning stations about *Bud, Not Buddy* and who introduced me to a whole new way to be a librarian.

Angie Branyon, Shannon Smith, and Carolyn Stenzel, each of whom co-created one of the example sets of learning stations that appear in this book.

Judi Repman, acquisitions editor at Libraries Unlimited, for her guidance, suggestions, and admirable patience with my many questions.

Ann M. Martin, who graciously provided the foreword for this book, and who has always been the ultimate library rock star.

The librarians of Henrico County Public Schools, for all of their support and constant inspiration.

And finally, I am deeply grateful to my family: my parents for always building me up, and Jamie, Paige, and Lila, for supporting me and sharing me while on this adventure. They made it through many a dinner without me, and picked up my household responsibilities so that I could write. It is because of them that this book exists. I am incredibly lucky to have their love and support.

Introduction

When I first became a librarian 10 years ago, I was given the exciting and rare opportunity to open the library at a brand new school. I loved being able to buy brand new books, choose a library assistant, and make suggestions during the building of the library itself. What excited me most though, was being able to create a library program from scratch.

I threw myself into the task with fervor. Our circulation statistics soared. My students wanted those new books! I began working on the climate by being positive and jovial with students, staff, and volunteers. People liked the library. But, I soon realized, other than checkouts, the library wasn't being used for research as much as I wanted or had anticipated. I counted nine research classes in a month. Nine, in a school of 900 students.

To boost the library program, I went to department meetings to show the teachers our databases, to talk about other resources, and to offer my services to them and their students. I began going to lunches in the workrooms with the teachers. When they would talk about what they were doing, I would promote ways in which I could help. The next month I counted fifteen research classes. Fifteen was not much of an improvement.

Obviously, I needed to do more. I began a research raffle. Each month at our faculty meeting, I would put all the names of the teachers who had research lessons with me in a hat, and I draw out a winner. The winner would get a $10 gift certificate. I justified this expense as necessary, because it was only $90 for the year, and would hopefully increase programming and book circulation. I figured I would get more teachers and students to use the library by spending $90 of my fundraising money that way, than if I had spent that same amount on six hardback books.

As I stood up in the meeting with a big smile on my face, I talked about what we could offer in the library, and what we had done for research over the past month. The talk was brief—shorter than five minutes. The next month I had 25 research classes. My program was growing!

For the next three years, my program grew, and I continued the raffle. I was up to 60 or so research classes a month, and I was thrilled! And . . . I was beginning to get bored.

"Here are the databases, this is how you use them, and this is why you use them. Here are some other great resources . . ." I felt as if I was doing the same lesson over and over with the English, science, and history classes. I needed something new, something that would still encourage growth, yet spice up the monotony of what I came to think of as my "general" lesson. I became a librarian with the idea of teaching all subjects to all grade levels, which was exciting. I was not interested in monotony.

At the end of my third year as a librarian, a teacher came to me and asked if I had ever created various stations for students. She wanted to have four or five stations of books set up and the kids could look for information at each one. She said she had a librarian in summer school who did that for a lesson for her. That librarian happened to be my mentor, Heather Gilbert Brandenburg, an innovative librarian who taught me much. I contacted her and she was willing share the content for a couple of stations she had created. I was intrigued.

As I thought more about this idea, I began to think about all the resources we could access using this model of research. Students could learn to use the resources while gathering information. I could use this approach to meet the AASL standards, as well as the teacher's state-mandated subject standards. A win for the teacher. A win for me. I hoped that in trying this format of teaching information-seeking and -retrieval strategies, that I would be able to create the positive dispositions within my students that I was ultimately aiming for. The more they used the sources, the more comfortable they would become, and the more likely they would be to use them again. I was ready to try it.

The first set of stations I used were for *Bud, Not Buddy* by Christopher Paul Curtis. I used some of the stations from Heather, and created a few of my own. A lot of books, a database, and some websites were used. The next set I created were from scratch, on the Vietnam War. They, too, were book heavy, but I added some primary source footage, war protest songs, a podcast of a veteran's story, a database, and a website as well. I enjoyed them, my students enjoyed them, and the teacher really enjoyed them. I felt like I was on to something that could help students meet my goals as well as their teachers' goals. I had much to learn about using this multimedia learning station method, and many more stations ahead of me.

This book is written for middle and high school librarians. It focuses on creating a library program that uses multimedia learning stations to increase information literacy skills within content and standards-based education. They are not centers. Learning stations are not designed to be set up around the library for a student to go to if they want information or need to learn how to do something. Each set of multimedia learning stations are specifically designed to address a subject standard being taught within the classroom.

The first half of this book explains what multimedia learning stations are, the reasons for doing them, when to use them, how to use them, and how to create them. There are practical steps to take when creating them, and tried-and-true organizational techniques. Information on different types of multimedia learning stations and where to find good sources for each type of multimedia are also included. This first half of the book is meant to fully empower secondary (middle and high school) librarians to collaborate with their teachers to create their own sets of multimedia learning stations.

The second half of the book contains fully created sets of multimedia learning stations that can be used in a secondary school library. They have been used, modified, updated, and practiced in my own school library. There are numerous examples for all four core subject areas: English, math, science, and social studies. In addition to the activities and mini lessons at each station, complete with directions and questions, each example set also includes recommended grade level, subject standards, AASL standards, materials needed, pre-assessment and post-assessment questions, and an idea for a larger research project extension to use after the lesson has been conducted in the library.

I hope that this book will set you on an exciting path that will brighten your day with variety, facilitate instruction for your students, strengthen the overall research process in your schools, and help you form productive, collaborative partnerships with your school's teachers.

Part I

Theory and Methodology

1

What Are Multimedia Learning Stations?

Change Is Necessary

In schools across the nation, libraries are suffering from downsizing of staff and resources. Implementing multimedia learning stations is one way to prove the instructional usefulness of the librarian, while providing a way to teach students to become information literate. Using this process will increase a librarian's interactions with and influence on students, as well as increase the amount of collaboration they have with teachers in all content areas. It will also provide the data needed to present solid arguments to all stakeholders as to why school librarians are vital.

For the last two decades, school librarians have been fighting the "Keeper of the Books" stereotype. It is important, in this time of budget cuts and tight spending, to be viewed as more than just research experts. School librarians are master teachers who must be versed in all content areas. They need to lead the charge and be equipped to inject any subject with research, technology, 21st-century skills, and real-world connections. It is through these methods that school librarians will become indispensable.

To change the mindset of our stakeholders, and increase our interactions with students and collaboration with teachers, schools need to offer a new method of instruction. It is time to expand the concept of teaching information literacy, and to inject research into content curricula, rather than teaching the research process in isolation or purely within the context of stand-alone research projects.

The Basics

Multimedia learning stations are activity- and standards-based, research-focused learning stations that students rotate through in order to learn more about a subject they are studying in the classroom. At each learning station, students implement a different kind of resource in order to research an aspect of the overall theme or unit of study.

Each learning station addresses the essential questions that have been developed for the content. Some of the forms of resources students utilize while working in multimedia learning stations include databases, websites, podcasts, videos, books, eBooks, encyclopedias, educational apps, music, and photographs. The stations also provide an excellent opportunity to present students with primary and secondary sources, and to help them learn the difference between the two.

An alternative to direct instruction, multimedia learning stations provide students with an opportunity to learn how to manipulate multiple resources, gain practice using them, and to seek help when they need it. By experiencing this facilitative learning environment full of ongoing research, students are able to strengthen their understanding of the research process and to build positive dispositions that make them more information literate, well-versed in 21st-century skills, and better prepared for doing independent research in future. Differentiation for each student, based on his or her learning needs, occurs naturally in this environment.

> Jen's model for creating integrated, resource-rich stations is simply the best structure for collaborating with teachers from *any* content area. Jen's stations start by unpacking the curriculum objectives to identify relevant driving questions, layering in the American Association of School Librarians' (AASL's) *Standards for the 21st-Century Learner* to support critical thinking and inquiry, and taking it home by creating independent, easily differentiated learning experiences where students can self-evaluate and reflect on their learning. Her stations have inspired me to look for more interactive ways to introduce students to various resources, while engaging them with multiple formats such as video, music, images, and primary source documents. After learning from the *best*, I have been able to translate Jen's framework for stations to multiple content areas that resonate with students of all ages.
>
> — Shannon Hyman, librarian

> I love stations! They help me learn about a topic in an interactive way that helps me understand what we're learning about. The stations give you a chance to delve deeper into a topic. They really are fun and helpful when it comes to remembering and discovering new information.
>
> — Dani, student

Interdependent Learning Process

Each AASL *Standards for the 21st-Century Learner* includes skills, dispositions, responsibilities, and self-assessment strategies. These four categories flow in and out of each other, and all are needed for optimal learning. Multimedia learning stations allow students the opportunity to build and practice skills, establish positive dispositions, take on more responsibilities, and create meaningful student self-assessment strategies.

As skills are being practiced, new habits are being formed, which helps students to take more responsibility for their learning. Self-assessment occurs during the process to ensure that students are learning effective skills, creating positive research habits, and taking on responsibilities for their learning. Weaknesses determined through self-assessment can be addressed and strengthened. Multimedia learning stations create a setting for establishing an interdependent learning process.

Core Subjects Targeted

Multimedia learning stations are targeted specifically toward core subject standards in English, math, science, and social studies. Each learning station attacks a different subject standard while requiring students to employ 21st century and information literacy skills.

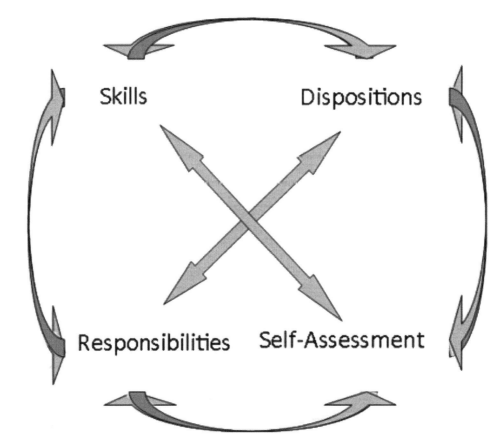

Interdependent learning process

Learning stations are different than library centers. Centers tend to concentrate on one skill in isolation. Multimedia learning stations have students learn research skills within the content and standards of their subject area. Instead of having a center for learning how to use the eBook collection, students will look for a specific eBook, with information pertaining to the particular standard they are researching. If they are researching natural resources, and the eBook learning station is about oil resources, students may download a book about fracking to find that specific information.

This practice has students learn how to download an eBook, practice using it, and execute a keyword search within it. Plus, they enhance their curricular knowledge about the topic they are researching—in this case, fracking. The information they find in the eBook will target specific subject standards students are required to know for that class, as well as address the AASL standards that will improve their independent research process in the future.

> Stations give us the opportunity to learn something new.
>
> — Lizzie, student

Facilitative in Nature

Collaborating with the teacher of the content area and integrating the state standards is crucial for creating effective learning stations. Twenty-first century technology and information literacy skills should not be taught in isolation, but within the context of other learning. Once students have used an eBook effectively at a learning station, they have learned the subject standard through facilitative

Exploring an eBook for information on fracking

instruction, and are more likely to check out an eBook on their own for personal reading or research in future visits. Students are exposed to different types of multimedia resources, which enhances the content they learn through self-guided practice.

In order for the facilitative structure of learning stations to succeed, directions have to be clear, teachers and librarians need to be available for assistance, and the use of both group work and independent work must be employed. Many students prefer to ask how to do something, rather than to read directions and exercise independent strategies on their own. In order to address this issue and encourage students to think through problems, a "Try Three Before You Ask Me" policy can be implemented. Students must double- and triple-check all directions and try on their own three times before they can ask for help.

It is a tough practice for them to grasp at the beginning. When a student raises a hand to ask for help, rather than explaining the learning station directions step-by-step, the librarian can assist them in breaking down the steps of finding what they need by walking them through the questioning process they should be using to navigate through their difficulties.

Here is an example of a typical first conversation with a student who hasn't yet learned how to problem solve for a task:

> Student: I need help.
> Librarian: Did you try the directions three times first?
> Student: Yes.
> Librarian: OK. What can I help you with?
> Student: This.
> Librarian: Please be more specific.
> Student: This right here.

Establish Dispositions

Every teacher and librarian has experienced the above scenario. It is important at this point to walk students through the processes they should be using to problem solve on their own, rather than to solve the problem for them. Establishing these key dispositions in our students is one of the librarian's ultimate goals, but students need to actually be trained in the process in order to be successful. The conversation will then tend to continue as follows:

> Librarian: Look at what is confusing you and form a specific question about what you need help with that doesn't include me doing it for you.
> Student: Can you help me with these directions?
> Librarian: Sure. What is the last step in the directions you completed?
> Student: Ummm…
> Librarian: Show me the last one you did and read to me what comes next.
> Student: I did step three last.
> Librarian: OK. Read step four.
> Student: Oh! I see it now!

It is often that simple. It can take a long time to get them to walk through the process, but they eventually learn that if no one will do it for them, they are able to backtrack and figure it out themselves.

When students need help understanding what a question is asking, the librarian and student can break it down, look up unknown words, and talk through the meaning together. Our students cannot be expected to learn to do this on their own, without proper guidance. Due to the facilitative nature of learning stations, students who have already established these dispositions can keep moving ahead, while those who haven't can receive assistance in learning self-questioning techniques.

> I like stations because it helps us to find new ways to research a topic.
>
> — Gina, student

Differentiation

These methods are a natural part of differentiation. According to Carol Tomlinson, in her article "Mapping a Route Toward Differentiated Instruction," differentiation must be centered in a classroom where there are equal parts student engagement and understanding. Only then can true learning occur. Standards-based curriculum and thoughtful essential questions should be the guide for all learning. Differentiation can then occur. She suggests knowing the ending before beginning instruction (Tomlinson, 1999). With the final goal in mind, teachers (and school librarians) can differentiate instruction for students to get to that final goal, based on their present needs.

The small-group environment allows teachers and school librarians to offer assistance and to be able to modify lessons and assignments to meet their goals. The library is the great equalizer for humanity, providing equal access to information for all. In school libraries, if students are to have equality in instruction and education, different methods must be applied that are specific to different students' needs and learning styles. Multimedia learning stations provide the opportunity for that differentiation, which leads to educational equality.

> I can't thank you enough for [the research class] today! The stations were so well thought-out, and presented in a manner that my special education students were able to be successful at doing research. When I gave the direction to clean up, one student who does very little work on a daily basis asked, "Can I just do one more?" She in fact did three more. It was a joy to participate in the 1960s stations!
>
> — Mrs. Levay, reading teacher

Summary

Multimedia learning stations are standards-based, rotating learning stations that focus on students' conceptual understandings of a topic's essential questions by employing multiple types of resources. Multimedia learning stations help middle school and high school librarians make inroads into the classroom. They are successful because they open the doors for collaboration with teachers, so that subject content learning is infused with 21st-century technology skills.

Students become information literate and learn their content within the context of the lesson. Through the implementation of these multimedia learning stations, instructions can be differentiated for individual students, and teachers have the opportunity to collaborate with the librarian in a new way. Often, teachers in a middle school or high school don't realize how the library can be helpful, or how the librarian can be of service. But once relationships have been established between the teacher and the librarian, the door to collaboration has opened. Teachers then feel more comfortable collaborating on research projects, as well as using multimedia learning stations.

> Stations gives us a chance to explore the topic in greater detail.
>
> — Alexis, student

These learning stations also aim to help students establish positive dispositions for the research processes they will apply independently in future. These learning stations are firmly grounded in the principles of 21st-century instruction, facilitative instruction, and student engagement, making real-world connections between classroom and everyday life.

> In the past, Mrs. Spisak has shared her vision with me. She told me, "I want the library to be the hub of the entire school, where everyone feels welcome and plugged in." Mrs. Spisak delivers on this by working diligently to develop rapport with the students and staff.
>
> She is especially adept at creating stations, which show students ways to think critically about a topic, and provide the students with important experience in utilizing media and library resources. Through the focus on facilitating instruction, students often state that they gained a new perspective on a topic. Students are inspired by the kinds of engaging activities she offers. She has now gone one step further, supporting instruction in the classroom after certain library visits, to keep the momentum of her lessons going!
>
> — Robbi Moose, principal

2

Reasons for Implementing Multimedia Learning Stations

Strengthen the Research Process

Although students today are generally considered to be digital natives, they are not research or learning natives. With guidance, however, they can become more familiar with these processes and develop into researching and learning immigrants who evaluate sources and extract essential knowledge.

> The stations expand our knowledge of research, while teaching us a lot about a certain topic.
>
> — April, student

When students use multimedia learning stations, they are strengthening their understanding of the research process. They build on skills they already have and create new dispositions, or habits of the mind, for future research. When students work through learning stations, they are using and exploring good sources of information. The practices acquired by researching the sources of information within each learning station increase the likelihood of their returning to the source again.

> When I teach a novel, I focus, of course, on the reading skills necessary to understand and enjoy the crafting of the English language. I try to choose books that have connections to other content areas the students are studying. Mrs. Spisak's stations are a wonderful way to expand content learning, and to allow students to really delve into a time period or a subject in ways I don't often have time for in the classroom. For example, Mrs. Spisak developed library stations for the book *Crispin: The Cross of Lead* by Avi. Students learned all about the issues facing people of the medieval era in Europe, and could thereby visualize what is described in our novel and truly understand the history! And, students are amazed and enjoy the learning!
>
> — Susan Loan, English teacher

Students get exposed to multiple types of sources. During research lessons, for example, students are exposed to sources such as databases and books and reminded to use them. In multimedia learning stations, they actively use them to research information at each learning station. It is an excellent opportunity for students to use primary and secondary sources found in a variety of formats (print and digital). Students can access these sources through databases, websites, educational apps, streaming videos, podcasts, books, and encyclopedias.

Exploring database search results at a multimedia learning station on bacteria

Use Facilitative Instruction

Using multimedia learning stations allows a librarian to switch from the role of didactic instructor to that of facilitator. Learning stations offer a platform that enables librarians to either create real-world problems students must solve, or to offer real-world sources of information they can use to construct new knowledge. Such a platform makes it possible for students to navigate information and build positive dispositions for research.

Students are able to use information they find to grasp the meaning of it on their own. Librarians guide them through the resources to use and the steps to take, so that they can ultimately extract meaning from what they find. This approach allows for less direct instruction but provides more guidance. The goal is to gradually decrease student dependence on an instructor.

This scaffolding involves guiding students through the processes that will become instinctive and allowing them to research both independently and effectively. We can take students through questions they have by using questioning and modeling, in order to help them develop the skills and dispositions they should have for lifelong, independent research.

> I like stations because they are fun and interactive.
>
> — Amanda, student

There needs to be a shift in our libraries. Librarian-centered teaching needs to give way to student-centered learning. Students need to become more active participants in their learning, rather than remaining relegated to the passive role they are accustomed to during direct instruction. The librarian and teacher shift from didactic style teaching to designing a method of learning where students work to find information rather than passively receiving it.

Student Engagement and Immersion in Subject

When students are engaged in their learning, they perform, learn, and understand better. Students remember more when their curiosity is sparked, and when they have the opportunity to explore their own creative and original thoughts. The multimedia learning station format helps students become engaged in their learning through music, visuals, and interactive games. They then can take the information they've learned through a variety of forms, think about it, create something from it, share it with others, and grow through the process.

> The beauty of a station is that a large topic can be broken down and chunked into more manageable pieces for students. Students stay engaged during a station activity, since they accomplish tasks in a short amount of time before traveling to the next station.
>
> — Jenna Szot, history teacher

Immersing students in a subject using songs, video, images, and interactive games, as well as textual information, piques their

> Stations are very engaging and useful when you want to understand a specific subject.
>
> — Katie, student

> My students love using stations in the library. Being able to use primary resources, do hands on activities, or immerse themselves in the culture of a time period through music, etc., really brings our topics to life. Students are engaged and involved so much more than in just the regular classroom.
>
> — Suzanne Stockman, history teacher

> Stations are an interactive, engaging, and fun way to learn new information for a subject!
>
> — Roman, student

interest and allows them to think about it in new ways. Using primary sources whenever possible adds a sense of reality to the lesson for them. For instance, when students read letters exchanged between the home front and the front lines of the American Revolution, it brings a new reality to the subject. Students can read the letters and create a text message that would be sent using a cell phone to deliver the same message if it were sent today. This gets students to read, comprehend, organize, and concisely deliver the overall essence of the letters. Students remain completely engaged throughout this activity, and consequently, they remember it and grow from it.

Builds Collaborative Partnerships

> Prior to coming to Hungary Creek, students expressed a lack of interest when visiting the library. Visiting the library was never a journey but a task, at previous schools. Until Jenifer Spisak encouraged me to give it one more try. Well, the rest is "History." I now visit the library at least once every nine weeks. Mrs. Spisak takes the lessons and brings them to life with the station activities. The theme of the lesson inspires the transition music, station numbers, video segments, and much more! Thank you, Mrs. Spisak, for making the library a visual journey!
>
> — Lakisha Greenhow, history teacher

> Jen's stations, created for the novels I teach in the classroom, allow us to collaborate and have students explore additional themes from the book, using a variety of technology as resources.
>
> — Shelly Barnard, English teacher

> My students love to work in stations because it gives them the opportunity to work collaboratively in small groups with their peers. It makes research, problem-solving, and critical thinking more engaging and fun.
>
> — Kathy Richardson, science teacher

Being a librarian with a thriving, successful library program requires collaboration between the librarian and each of the school's stakeholders: students, teachers, administration, and the community. Using multimedia learning stations is a way to create collaborative partnerships. The type of lessons that stem from this synergy are naturally collaborative. Teachers want to work with a librarian who wants to work within their curriculum.

When teachers like the lessons and feel involved with the content being taught in the library, they come more often. The more they come, the busier the library program becomes. They talk about the library program with other teachers, in and out of the building. They begin advocating for the library, talking about what makes it great and necessary. Eventually, the administration sees how busy the library is. After talking with administrators about what goes on in the library and inviting them to observe, they begin to advocate and discuss the library program at their school as a bragging point.

Meanwhile, parents notice that students are using the library more. Parent volunteers speak about the library and what goes on there. Before long, all stakeholders in the school community begin advocating for the library. Effective collaboration between these stakeholders and the librarian helps build the program and generates widespread endorsement of it.

Opportunities for Group and Independent Work

The world has dramatically changed in the last few decades, to one that is increasingly collaborative. This shift has become especially evident in the workplace, where more emphasis is placed on working as a team. Students need to begin preparing for this work world by learning to work together while in the school setting. Multimedia learning stations provide a natural way for students to work together as a group, and to work independently. Regardless of whether students work better alone or in a group, it is necessary that they acquire experience in both types of learning situations.

At one set of learning stations, students may have the opportunity to work together, discussing ideas and helping one another. At other learning stations, they may have to rely on themselves to find information and to critically work through it. Often they can learn questioning and thought techniques from each other at group work learning stations that they can subsequently apply at individual work learning stations, where the facilitative instructor can provide assistance and gather assessments based on careful observation and questioning of students.

> Stations give me a chance to interact with people I see every day, but don't really talk to.
> — Anna, student

Students working as a group to identify the parts of a cell

Variety of Topics and Multiple Resources

A variety of subtopics within a larger topic can be explored during multimedia learning stations. This capability provides students with an excellent opportunity to experience multiple points of view on one topic, such as gun control, or the reasons colonists would have supported or not supported the American Revolution. Being able to access multiple topics and points of view keeps students interested and engaged.

In these "multiple points of view" lessons, a variety of resources are used. Students are exposed to sources that are more substantial than a Google search or a Wikipedia article. Specifically, they are familiarized with the subscription databases they are encouraged to use. Additionally, they use more reliable websites, video streaming services, and podcasts from reliable sources such as National Public Radio (NPR). Exploring and using multiple resources for a variety of topics gives students exposure and practice using reliable information. Once they have used and practiced with multiple resources, they are more likely to return to them for independent research later.

Working independently on an interactive website to learn about the immigrant experience at the turn of the 20th century

> Stations provide my students the opportunity to experience a large number of resources in a short period of time. Stations not only help students learn the material. They also become better learners and researchers.
> — Ellen Jewell, history teacher

> There are different activities to do.
> — Madison, student

Meet the Needs of Students, Teachers, and Librarians by Reinforcing Curriculum and Supporting Standards

> Stations chunk down content standards into smaller more manageable sections, which helps students explore a variety of materials. Students move through the stations in small groups versus whole class instruction, fostering their need to ask questions, observe, think critically, and share knowledge. Using the AASL standards, librarians use student-centered learning stations to put ownership back into the student's hands and allow them to take risks without fear of failure.
>
> — Alison Timm, librarian and former English teacher

Multimedia learning stations are constructed in collaboration with a classroom teacher using the curriculum subject standards and the AASL *Standards for the 21st-Century Learner*. Since the AASL standards concentrate on skills, dispositions, responsibilities, and self-assessment strategies, they mesh easily with a lesson for any curriculum. Data and standardized testing are a mandatory part of public education; the role of the librarian is to educate the whole child and to help them achieve academic success.

Students need to be able to pass the standardized tests at the end of the year, teachers need to cover all of their course material, and librarians need to teach research and information-seeking strategies. This process ensures that the needs of everyone are being met while employing 21st-century and critical thinking skills.

Students are provided with the opportunity to move during a multimedia learning stations activity. Research has shown that physical movement stimulates different parts of the brain (Jensen, 2005). Having a new place to go every 10 to 15 minutes gives students a brief physical and mental break from what they are doing. This keeps them more engaged in their activities. Students don't have the opportunity to zone out and lose part of the lesson, because they are constantly moving, researching using different sources, and exploring different topics.

Students enjoy this movement from one learning station to the next, and often dance their way as they go. Playing music specific to the topic in some way gives them the opportunity to experience their movement and the learning stations in a completely different way. They often comment that the movement is one of the parts they like the best, because they can let out some energy along the way.

Students work together to construct a scaled model of the Willis Tower

Provide an Opportunity to Make Real-World Connections

Multimedia learning stations provide the opportunity to bring in the real world. Students often have a tough time connecting their studies to the world they live in. Learning stations can help foster such connections and, by extension, make the lessons more meaningful. It is also a great way to introduce students to new technologies and Web 2.0 platforms.

When English students read *The Giver* by Lois Lowry, they are introduced to a dystopian society. They learn the difference between utopian and dystopian societies in class, but sometimes have a difficult time understanding that both types of societies often started with the same goal: perfection. In *The Giver* multimedia learning stations, students explore present-day ideas, societies, and experiments in our culture that began as a way to try to achieve perfection. Students can discuss and explore the ethics of these ideas and societies. They can research communes and communal living using the subscription databases, cloning using a subscription video streaming service, North Korea using a podcast, biodômes and climate-control using the website from the Montreal Biodôme, Amish culture using databases, and China's one-child policy using books and eBooks.

Students are able to explore these topics in detail and to react to them; for each of these ideas and societies, students think critically about both the positive and negative impacts. They work together in groups and have thoughtful discussions as they go. The fact that each of these ideas and types of societies exist in today's world gives them a lot to think about and discuss, such as how each pertains to *The Giver*, how each was created, and what each has become. (See *The Giver* Learning Stations)

Multimedia learning stations can be used to explore probability, percents, ratios, and proportions, allowing students a look at jobs and life situations that are fun. At one learning station, students are architects, using a website for the Willis Tower to determine its dimensions and use proportion, to create a scale that they then build with Tinker Toys. At a second learning station, they act as political analysts, using the atlas to see the voting trends of their state's presidential elections over the last hundred years, and then using these statistics to calculate the odds of how their state will vote in the next election. At a third learning station, students act as sports analysts, using videos from the Discovery Education subscription streaming service to make the connection that baseball batting average and basketball free-throw percentages are pure probability. At a fourth learning station, students use the databases to learn about and practice the theory of probability by playing Go Fish, with an added hint for one lucky player. At the final learning station, students pretend to be game show contestants who use probability, math, and library books to solve the game-winning question. Students enjoy these learning stations immensely, especially getting to be architects who build towers out of Tinker Toys. (See Probability, Percents, Ratios, and Proportions Learning Stations)

> Using Tinker Toys and directive websites, students experience real-world examples of how today's engineers use proportional reasoning to design and construct our skyscrapers.
>
> — Jane Williams, math teacher and gifted student program coordinator

Address Multiple Intelligences and Multiple Learning Styles

Howard Gardner's theory of multiple intelligences describes the way people mentally compute information (Gardner, 1983), whereas Rita Dunn and Ken Dunn's theory of multiple learning styles focuses on the ways people prefer to approach information (Dunn & Dunn, 1978). Each individual person can possess multiple intelligences, but each typically favors one learning style over the other.

The multiple intelligences are intrapersonal, interpersonal, logical-mathematical, naturalist, spatial, bodily-kinesthetic, linguistic, and musical. Good multimedia learning stations include most of these intelligences; since students hold multiple intelligences, it helps to address as many of them as possible. Multiple learning styles encompass auditory learners, visual learners, and kinesthetic learners. Likewise, good multimedia learning stations should vary from station to station with regard to the style in which information is presented. Learners will have the chance to practice and get help from other students at learning stations that are presented in the learning styles they are weakest in. Since students hold multiple intelligences, it helps to address as many of them as possible.

Multiple intelligences and multiple learning styles are addressed by the variety of research sources used in multimedia learning stations, as well as the ways in which information is presented, and the ways in which students are asked to process, understand, and evaluate information. Some learning stations require students to read and work with text from websites, databases, or print resources. Others

> Stations are helpful to all children with different learning styles.
>
> — Christy, student

> The stations that are done at the library are the perfect way to use multiple intelligences and differentiated instruction. It also really helps to distinguish class leaders. It is great for students to see that books, magazines, and newspapers are still used for research, and *not* only the internet!
>
> — Mrs. Sommers, reading teacher

> It lets you learn in ways you like to learn, and shows you new ways to learn.
>
> — Riley, student

employ auditory elements using podcasts, videos, or music. And still others focus on more kinesthetic options involving manipulatives.

Learning stations can use maps from websites or print sources, or, to address those who are more spatially oriented, use more interactive maps such as Google Earth. Using both group and individual work in learning stations addresses intrapersonal and interpersonal learning styles. Having students analyze patterns or calculate math in real and natural ways addresses logical and mathematical intelligences. Through learning stations, students have plenty of opportunity to use verbal, auditory, and kinesthetic styles.

Provide Opportunity to Differentiate Instruction

No two students learn the same way (Tomlinson, 1999). On her website, Carol Tomlinson states that differentiated instruction is "an approach to teaching that advocates active planning for student differences in classrooms" (Tomlinson, 2013, para. 1).

Multimedia learning stations address student differences in numerous ways. In addition to confronting multiple learning styles and offering a variety of topics for multiple intelligences, multimedia learning stations provide the means for differentiated instruction. For example, librarians and teachers can build in more small group or one-on-one opportunities for students who need extra help breaking down instructions and learning how to use higher-level thinking skills. Moreover, they can modify the learning station activity to best accommodate an individual student's learning needs.

Diane Ravitch states in her book, *EdSpeak: A Glossary of Education Terms, Phrases, Buzzwords, and Jargon,* "In practice, [differentiated instruction] involves offering several different learning experiences in response to students' varied needs. Educators may vary learning activities and materials by difficulty, so as to challenge students at different readiness levels" (Ravitch, 2007, p. 75). Multimedia learning stations make it possible to vary learning stations for different students, based on their needs.

Build Library Program and Increase Usage and Collaboration with Teachers

Implementing the use of multimedia learning stations will increase the usage of a library within any school. Teachers want to work with librarians who help them teach their curriculum. When teachers are in the library with their classes more frequently, the usage statistics of the library go up, and because students are in the library more often, circulation goes up, and database usage increases. The number of research classes is consequently elevated, so the library program grows. The result is a library that is more active, vibrant, and busier.

They're FUN!

Multimedia learning stations can be fun. Because these learning stations incorporate different topics and sources, and because they add kinesthetic learning stations, rotations, and music, students become more engaged. Students are intrigued and energized by the opportunity to solve real-world problems, and feel the purpose for the day is validated. They state that these lessons are more fun than regular lessons. They enjoy being interactive with their learning and, in turn, learn more because of it.

> The stations are my favorite academic thing to do for school.
>
> — Brian, student

> Stations are fun and always help me to learn.
>
> — Taylor, student

> I enjoy stations and I am always happy when we go to the library, because I enjoy all the different kinds of activities, and they are so much fun!!
>
> — Jake, student

3

Types of Multimedia Learning Stations

Many different types of multimedia learning stations can be used within a created set. It is important to add variety and to create learning stations that engage multiple intelligences. Stations that have variety keep students focused, and ones that address multiple intelligences enable them to practice and acquire new skills and dispositions. This chapter focuses on different types of individual learning stations that can be created, and good sources of information for each type.

Databases

Databases are subscription services that contain a variety of sources of information from professionals. They include articles from magazines, encyclopedias, newspapers, and journals. Books, or excerpts of books, can also be found in databases. The information is deemed reliable, but students should be taught to always question what they read anywhere, and to check multiple sources of information for verification. Database learning stations can be set up on computers for students to share, on personal laptops for students with a 1:1 computer initiative, or on tablets or other handheld devices.

Schools tend to subscribe to their preferred databases from particular companies, based on what the school needs and can afford. Researching within these databases should always be encouraged. Some common companies that offer numerous databases are Gale, ABC-CLIO, EBSCO Information Services, ProQuest, and Britannica Academic. Plenty of other reliable, user-friendly databases also exist, and should be researched to see which ones match the needs of a school or an entire district.

In addition to what a school provides, states usually provide access to certain databases through the public libraries. These databases can be made available to students as well. For instance, sometimes schools partner with the public libraries to share databases. Students can use their public library card at school to access these databases, and some public libraries will even offer a library card to a school for students to use as a group. Collaboration between the school and public libraries maximizes students' database access.

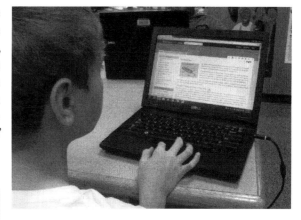

Exploring a database article for information

Podcasts or Audio Files

Podcasts or audio files include radio broadcasts, audio files from taped interviews, and podcasts people create to stream on the web, as well as anything that provides just audio. These audio sources are now ubiquitous. Some good sources for audio are listed below.

National Public Radio (NPR) (www.npr.org). NPR has a vast amount of podcasts and radio broadcasts available through streaming on their website. They often include primary footage from historical time periods and interviews with people whom students are studying. Students can listen to interviews with American soldiers in a concentration camp the day it was liberated, while the prisoners sing with joy and relief in the background. They can listen to a speech by Martin Luther King Jr., or a story by a Vietnam veteran about the difficulty of returning to the United States after the war. In addition to audio, NPR offers the written transcript for many of its broadcasts. This option tends to benefit students who struggle with the auditory learning style.

Databases. Subscription databases often contain audio files with primary and secondary source material.

Apps on iOS devices: iTunes U and Podcasts. Both the iTunes U and Podcasts apps have easily searchable podcast databases for lessons. Both can be accessed on iOS devices that the library owns or during a Bring Your Own Device (BYOD) lesson.

Julie DeNeen's online article "50 Educational Podcasts You Should Check Out" also provides many sources for podcasts from a multitude of subject areas. http://gettingsmart .com/2013/02/50-educational-podcasts-you-should-check-out/

Podcasts are best listened to individually, but if there are not enough computers or devices to make this possible, headphone splitters can connect up to five pairs of headphones to one device. The podcast can also be played aloud for the group members to hear, provided that the learning station is located far enough away from other students to prevent it being a distraction.

Using the iCell app to distinguish the differences between plant and animal cells

Educational Apps

Educational Apps are applications built for tablets and other handheld devices. Countless educational apps exist for iOS and android devices. These apps can be found in the Apple App Store, for iOS devices, or through the Google Play store or the Amazon Appstore, for Android devices. Exploring these stores can provide many results. Each store has an education category, which is an obvious place to find relevant apps. However, some of the best apps can be found by simply searching through the store for the subject being taught.

There are different types of apps for learning station activities. Some offer methods of finding information through text, others present information nestled within colorful or fun visuals that bring content to life, and still others teach students by having them play games. Each of these methods holds value and can add to a lesson by increasing student engagement and knowledge of a subject area.

Many of the educational apps are free for educators. Unfortunately, there are also many notable apps that are not free. People debate whether or not to spend the money on educational apps. Quite frankly, some of them are just worth the price. Some of the apps that are worth the price of purchase include Britannica, National Geographic, and Kids Discover. They have information that can apply to many sets of learning stations, because they have vast amounts of information and are fairly easy to search and navigate.

> Apple usually has a deal in August/September of each year. If you buy an iPad or iPad Mini, you get a free $50 gift card to Apple's App Store. I try to buy an iPad Mini each September, using the education discount, to take advantage of the deal. I use these gift cards to purchase apps and music for my multimedia learning stations.

Some of the best apps are subject specific. By searching through the multitude of options, an app can be found for most lessons. It can help to have students practice with the apps, to see if they would be easy to learn and play within the short timeframe of a learning station. Kids stopping by the library really enjoy trying these out. The following are some quality, free education apps to begin an app collection. These apps can apply to many subject areas but do not negate the need to search for other subject-specific apps.

App learning stations can be run either with each individual student having a tablet or hand-held device or with two or more students sharing devices. On apps that have sound, more than one pair of headphones can be connected to a device, using a headphone splitter to contain the noise. Employing a Bring Your Own Device (BYOD) system could be effective for such a learning station. The school library might still have to provide headphones.

- Curious
- iBooks
- iCell
- iTunes U
- Khan Academy
- NASA
- NOVA Elements
- NPR Music
- Science360
- SimplePhysics
- SkyORB
- Solve the Outbreak
- TED
- TinkerBox

Videos

Video clips provide a visual for students that allows them to gather information and be submerged in a subject area. Videos can be primary source footage, such as a news report from the Vietnam War,

Students watching a short video clip to visualize and learn their class's content material

or they can simply be a mode of presenting information for students to collect. Videos that are six minutes or shorter tend to be best for learning stations. Clips of this length give students time to get to a video, watch it, and answer questions.

Video learning stations tend to be either informational or thought provoking. When the primary focus of the learning station is to gather information, the questions asked are lower on Bloom's Taxonomy scale, and students should be encouraged to collect this information as they go. When the purpose of the video station is to provoke thought, students should be encouraged to watch the video in its entirety, and then either have a discussion about it with group members, or think about it on their own and answer thought questions. The discussion and thought questions address the higher levels of Bloom's Taxonomy scale (Bloom, 1956), (Anderson & Krathwohl, 2001).

Print resources are good sources of information as well

Discovery Education is a subscription video service. It is expensive, but well worth the money when designing multimedia learning stations. Its videos cover diverse subjects, are broken down by grade level and category, and are even searchable by full video or video segment. The videos in Discovery Education come from a wide array of media and educational sources. The service also includes citations for each video in its extensive collection.

BrainPOP is another video subscription service. It is more appropriate for middle school than for high school students, but it presents information on all subjects through animation. Students find it to be quirky and fun. BrainPOP also has quizzes at the end of a video, if a librarian or teacher chooses to make them a part of the learning station.

Most subscription databases have videos that can be accessed during multimedia learning stations. This option is a good way to provide information and to have students practice searching the databases. Students learn to navigate the databases to find information through text, video, audio, and images. Many students aren't aware that the databases provide more than print text. Another advantage is that, because the videos are found in the databases, most of their citations have already been created and are available in the database.

WatchKnowLearn (http://www.watchknowlearn.org) is a domain that houses more than 50,000 educational videos. The videos are organized by subject and age level of students. The videos on this website are submitted by educators and then reviewed and selected by the Watch Know Learn staff.

Believe it or not, YouTube (https://www.youtube.com/), TeacherTube (http://www.teachertube .com/), and YouTube EDU (https://www.youtube.com/t/education) can be sources of good videos.

Students need to understand the difference between a good video source and a poor quality one. Videos that are posted to display student projects and random individuals' thoughts should prompt discussions about sources that are unreliable or of low quality.

On the other hand, people posting to YouTube can also publish videos from national news networks or from other reliable people or organizations. Because YouTube is blocked in many schools and having students searching through YouTube isn't a best practice, videos can be downloaded through websites such as KeepVid. The video can then be watched through a central computer or an information sharing system such as Blackboard. Questions can then be asked as to why the video itself is a good source. Librarians will need to make sure to stay within copyright laws, which vary depending on the video chosen. An additional benefit to these sources is that their videos can be accessed for free.

Major networks such as ABC, CBS, NBC, and PBS all have video archives that can be explored and utilized within multimedia learning stations. The websites for these networks and the videos on these websites are free, and as sources, tend to be reliable. These videos can be streamed to one or more computers at the same time.

Video sources on the internet that can be explored are abundant. In addition to the previously mentioned options, some good places to find reliable video sources are the National Archives, NeoK12, TED, Khan Academy, Internet Archive, and iTunes U.

Students can view videos on personal computers while wearing headphones, to silence the sound for the rest of class. Videos can also be played using DVDs. A TV hooked up to a DVD player can be set up in a corner of the library as a learning station. If the noise from this learning station is too great, the video can be set up on a big screen and shown to the whole class at once. In this case, the class would complete this learning station together before rotating among the other learning stations.

Books and Encyclopedias: The UNmultimedia Learning Station

Although print books and encyclopedias aren't technically multimedia, they are still important sources of information for student research. It is important to offer a variety of sources when teaching students to be more information literate. Growing up in the digital age hasn't yet precluded the need for print resources. This learning station, within a set of multimedia learning stations, is the UNmultimedia learning station.

In addition to middle and high school level books, sometimes an approach through a children's picture book or a graphic novel can be a quick way to inform a student on a topic. Graphic Libraries has a line of content-based graphic novels that teach about historical people, places, and events. These books are excellent for giving information quickly and asking students to comment on what they learn.

> I explain to my students that sharing is give and take, and if someone in the group is only taking information without sharing anything they found for the group, then they are cheating. This discussion seems to be necessary with all grade levels, including twelfth graders.

The school library itself, as well as interlibrary loans from other school libraries, are the primary ways to locate print resources. The public library also has a variety of books that can be checked out by the librarian or the teacher and brought into the lesson. Any time additional copies of books are available, they should be provided. These print materials should be readily available at the learning station when students get there.

Print book and encyclopedia learning stations tend to require sharing of the materials among the group members. Often they divide the information being investigated between them, and share answers with one another. It would be beneficial to have a class discussion about the distinction between sharing and cheating before this type of station is created.

eBooks

Because eBooks can be used with computers, tablets, and handheld devices, they naturally fit into a set of multimedia learning stations. Learning to research these books for content will not only give students practice using eBooks, but will also give them the opportunity to see how to checkout an eBook for school assignments or for personal reading.

The public library and various websites offer ways to access eBooks in addition to the ones in a school library's collection. A negative aspect of implementing the public library's eBook collection in a learning station, is that students in a school setting must have a library card to access the collection. That said, some public libraries may be willing to issue a general library card to a school for the use of multimedia learning stations.

Project Gutenberg (http://www.gutenberg.org/) has well over 46,000 books that have been digitized into eBooks, and the website's collection is growing all the time. The Kindle Store and Barnes & Noble's NOOK store also provide access to many free books. Most of these books are in the public domain because they were published long ago, so they don't always provide the nonfiction information students seek in multimedia learning stations.

Both iBooks and Google Books provide access to thousands of free eBooks. They also provide access to excerpts of books that aren't available in their entirety. An excerpt of a book is often all a student needs to get information for a learning station. The excerpt of a book that Google Books provides will often give an account of an event that students can respond to during the learning station.

Learning to search through Google Books is especially beneficial for students, because it provides them with a technique for future research. It is easily accessible and full of relevant excerpts. Teaching students the process of conducting these searches in iBooks and Google Books is essentially providing them with a skill and knowledge of a very beneficial tool for research later.

Some additional websites that provide access to free eBooks are:

- Authorama - http://www.authorama.com

- Chest of Books - http://chestofbooks.com/

- eBook Lobby - http://www.ebooklobby.com/

- Open Library - https://openlibrary.org/ - an account must be created

- Questia - http://www.questia.com/library/free-books

During multimedia learning stations, eBooks can be viewed and read on computers that are shared or available for individual users, a tablet/eReader, or a handheld device. Many people have upgraded their eReaders over the years, and may be willing to donate their older versions to the school library. Asking parents for these donations in newsletters, the library blog, library social media tools, and PTA meetings may help a school library build an eReader collection. Because eBooks can be read on a multitude of devices, uniformity of the devices isn't important.

Websites

Websites are essential sources of information for multimedia learning stations. Often information can be found on reliable websites that cannot be found in other types of sources. Access to websites can be given to students in many ways. A collection of websites can be linked together for students to access through Web 2.0 tools, such as ThingLink or Symbaloo, which can then be shared with students. In addition to the option of offering a collection of websites, there is also the

Students use reliable websites for research

option of offering students one website for research in a particular learning station, or search strategies can be implemented using Google Advanced Search, Wolfram Alpha, or SweetSearch.

Using search engines effectively is a skill students need to learn. It is not a skill they possess inherently. When trying to conduct a search, students tend to type in a research question rather than keywords, or when they do retrieve results, they don't know which results are more reliable than others. Teaching students Google Advanced searching strategies at a learning station is teaching them a research skill that will benefit them throughout their school years. Students can learn to be specific in their searches, to look for keywords or phrases, and/or to limit a search to retrieve only ".gov" results when applicable.

Wolfram Alpha is a verified computational search engine that returns statistics and data for many topics. It even has a bit of a sense of humor similar to the iPhone's Siri. After typing "hello" in the search box and completing the search, Wolfram Alpha responds, "Hello, human." Humor aside, Wolfram Alpha is reliable in its statistics, and can even compare and contrast multiple items. SweetSearch is a search engine whose database has been stocked with reliable websites from educators around the world. Students like that it doesn't provide as many useless results as those offered by Google or Bing.

- Google Advanced Search - http://www.google.com/advanced_search

- Wolfram Alpha - http://www.wolframalpha.com/

- SweetSearch - http://www.sweetsearch.com/

There are several go-to websites for educational learning stations. In addition to those websites, there are numerous other websites available for all content areas. Best practice would be to search for the best websites for each new set of multimedia learning stations. That being said, listed below are some websites that are reliable sources of information for many topics.

- Britannica - http://www.britannica.com/

- Center for Disease Control (CDC) - http://www.cdc.gov/

- Digital Public Library of America - http://dp.la/

- Environmental Protection Agency (EPA) - http://www.epa.gov/

- How Stuff Works - http://www.howstuffworks.com/

- Library of Congress (LOC) - http://www.loc.gov/

- Media History Digital Library - http://mediahistoryproject.org/

- National Archives - http://www.archives.gov/

- National Geographic - http://www.nationalgeographic.com/

- NASA - http://www.nasa.gov/

- National Park Service (NPS) - http://www.nps.gov/

- Rock and Roll Hall of Fame - http://www.rockhall.com/

- Seriously Amazing (owned by Smithsonian) - http://seriouslyamazing.si.edu/

- Smithsonian - http://www.si.edu/

- White House - http://www.whitehouse.gov/

- The Why Files - http://whyfiles.org/

TED-Ed (http://ed.ted.com/) is a website put together by the creative geniuses of TED. It is a repository of lessons created around a TED Talk or any video from YouTube or elsewhere. These videos contain discussion questions and topics as well as supplemental materials. These lessons are put together by the team at TED or by anyone who wants to visit the website and create a lesson. They are useful in multimedia learning stations because a librarian can select a ready-made mini-lesson that fits with the topic students are exploring, or the librarian can create their own and upload it to the TED site. Students can select the link assigned to the lesson, explore it, experience it, and think through it.

To successfully employ websites during multimedia learning station, they should be viewed by two or more students on shared computers or by individual students on their own computers, if enough of them are available.

Online Games

Students love to interact with online games. Often games have students problem-solve and think critically about a topic they are researching. Some online games are more interactive than others. Games can be played with the purpose of reviewing, gathering information, interacting with a student's learning, or as a creative outlet for displaying learned knowledge.

The majority of online games for middle and high school students are most effectively played through educational apps. There are a few websites that provide content area games for older students, but more successful searching for these games is possible through educational apps.

Two subject specific websites with online games for middle and high school students are iCivics (https://www.icivics.org/) and My Garbology (http://www.naturebridge.org/garbology. php). iCivics was founded by retired U.S. Supreme Court Justice Sandra Day O'Connor, and has games that set up real-world problems for students to solve with the idea of making them good, responsible citizens in the world. My Garbology centers on what humans do with their waste. It shows students what to throw away, reuse, recycle, or compost, and what happens to waste when they do these things.

Many websites and blogs offer online games. Here are two that are helpful.

- http://www.sheppardsoftware.com/

- http://edtechideas.com/2009/12/21/60-educational-game-sites-that-you've-probably -never-seen/

Online games can best be played in groups or individually. For the games that have sound, a headphone splitter would be required to mute the sounds from the rest of the class.

Web 2.0 Tools

Adding the functions and the exploration of Web 2.0 tools to a learning station adds value to it. Through these tools, students learn a new information sharing platform, which gives them experience for future research projects.

Wordle created for a multimedia learning station on the history of the Harlem Renaissance

Padlet (http://padlet.com/) is a clever Web 2.0 tool that gives students a chance to share thoughts and information collaboratively. It is a blank wall on a computer screen on which students can add electronic post-it notes. Students like to share information and thoughts with each another in this manner. However, they must understand that what they write is public and available for the rest of the class to see. These walls of information can be password protected, so that only specific students are able to see the responses.

ThingLink (https://www.thinglink.com/) is a Web 2.0 platform that provides a way for teachers and/or students to share websites. A user selects an image for a topic and places links on the image that pertain to the topic being researched. The visual aspect of the picture makes the sharing of links more interesting than just providing a list.

Symbaloo (http://www.symbaloo.com/) serves the same function. A Symbaloo user can connect multiple websites to one central page. Students can be given the link to the initial Symbaloo page in order to have access to the links contained within it.

Animoto (http://animoto.com/) is a service that allows people to make mini music videos. Music is provided within the website that can be used without worry of copyright infringement, and students are able to type brief excerpts of text to go along with the images they post. Through Animoto, librarians can give information or show students how to do something, and students can demonstrate things they have learned. Products created with Animoto can serve as a form of assessment or as a method of displaying learning.

GoAnimate (http://goanimate.com/) can function in similar ways. Student can generate videos with the GoAnimate-provided voices, animated characters, and settings, rather than using music. Both of these tools require students to have an account to create something, but not to view what is already there.

Wordle (http://www.wordle.net/) is a word cloud generator. Students do not have to have an account to create with Wordle, but they do need to either learn to take a screenshot of any word cloud they create or to print it, because it cannot be saved. Wordle can consolidate information. It is a great tool to implement with biographies. If students are assigned to search the databases for a biography on

> It really helps me understand the topic more in a fun, productive way.
>
> — Maria, student

a historical figure, once they have found one, they can copy and paste the text from it into Wordle. A word cloud then returns with the words displayed in a cloud design. The words that appeared most often are bigger than the others. Through this method, students get a sense of the words that are most often associated with the particular person they are researching. With this tool, librarians can also create word clouds for each learning station, to demonstrate what the learning station will be about.

Glogster (http://edu.glogster.com/) allows users to create online posters. Students can demonstrate knowledge on a Glogster poster, which can be assessed, and librarians can also present information to students on a poster created in Glogster. An account is necessary in order to use this tool and create these posters. Education accounts are available that can be set up before multimedia lessons take place, but this service does cost a fee.

There are innumerable Web 2.0 tools available online, with more being created all the time. Librarians should explore what is out there and experiment with their findings. The American Association of School Librarians puts out a list of the 25 Best Websites for Teaching and Learning each year. They have been creating the list since 2009, and the websites and tools on it are very good. A compiled list of all the websites named on the lists since 2009 can be found at http://www.ala .org/aasl/standards-guidelines/best-websites/past.

Music

Music in multimedia learning stations sets the mood for the learning stations. If students are studying a historical time period or reading a book set in an earlier decade, the feel of the music of the time can bring another aspect of understanding to what they are researching. Music is usually implemented within one learning station, or as a means to signal the time to rotate to another learning station. This method can be performed with learning stations of all subject areas.

Executing multimedia learning stations in conjunction with the 1967 novel *The Outsiders* by S. E. Hinton provides an excellent opportunity to listen to music by Elvis Presley, the Beatles, and Bob Dylan, who are all mentioned in the book as being musical artists listened to in the 1960s, the era the story is set in. Students research biographical information on these musicians while listening to the music. After researching the details of these musicians' lives and listening to their music, students are then better able to determine why they think certain characters, each representing one of the socioeconomic statuses in the book, listen to the artists they do.

Specifically, they can make more informed judgments as to why the characters living in poorer conditions responded more to Elvis, while the wealthier characters chose to listen to the Beatles. Another example is when students in history classes have an opportunity to listen to Duke Ellington or Louis Armstrong while studying the Harlem Renaissance, or to play slow, mournful music when studying the Holocaust. Music is good for setting the mood, whether it pertains directly to the curriculum or not.

Music can be purchased by the school library. Alternatively, there are many music websites or applications that play short clips of music that can be used. Some sources for these clips of music are the iTunes Store, Amazon, and the AllMusic website (http://www.allmusic.com/).

Images

Images are powerful. They make it possible for students to get a clear picture of what it is they are researching. Images are available in apps, videos, websites, eBooks, and print sources. Encouraging students to use images in a learning station allows them time to observe and reflect upon what they are researching.

Student-created volcanoes built with Play-Doh to demonstrate understanding of different volcano shapes

An example of using images effectively in a learning station would be when studying the U.S. civil rights movement. This is an excellent time to have a learning station dedicated solely to images. Students can look at the pictures of sit-ins, marches, and children being sprayed with water hoses. They can see pictures of separate drinking fountains for whites and for African Americans. These images reinforce—even heighten—students' sense of awareness of the difficulties of that time. A learning station dedicated to images allows students time to look at the pictures, absorb them, analyze them, and reflect upon them.

Another option for incorporating images into a learning station is to have students pick an image for a particular time period, pretend to be a person in the picture, and write a first-person account of what they, as that person, are thinking and feeling in the picture.

Kinesthetic Activities

Kinesthetic activities can be integrated into many of the types of learning stations that have been mentioned. Building a skyscraper to scale with Tinker Toys, using information from a website about a skyscraper, can be an excellent way to teach students about proportions and scale. Having students learn about the three types of volcanoes from a website, then build those three types of volcanoes with Play-Doh demonstrates whether or not they truly understand the concept of volcanoes, appearances of volcanoes, and differences among the types of volcanoes. Believe or not, even eighteen-year-olds have fun molding and shaping Play-Doh to demonstrate their knowledge. (See Probability, Percents, Ratios and Proportions Learning Stations)

K'NEX produces many toys that can be built for use in lessons. Often these toys can be built ahead of time before a lesson, with or without student assistance, and the K'NEX models created can be used for other things as well. A K'NEX model truck ramp, with a truck that goes down it, can enhance the visualization and comprehension of a road manual's specifications for load-bearing trucks. It can also serve to demonstrate how the steepness of the slope of the road determines how much a truck can safely carry. (See Slope Learning Stations)

Having students learn and practice calligraphy can expand on the idea of calligraphy as being part of Chinese or Japanese culture, or even bring a section of the 1996 novel *The View from Saturday* by E. L. Konigsburg to life. Tea time traditions can be explored by having tea using the formal manners and tea etiquette that are proper according to *Emily Post's Etiquette*. Learning to play an authentic game of marbles the way Tom and Huck did can bring *The Adventures of Tom Sawyer* by Mark Twain to life. Most of today's students have never played a traditional game of marbles, and learning to play opens up a new realm of understanding for them. Any chance there is to combine a kinesthetic activity with a learning station benefits students.

> My students work so well in stations. The lessons are always put together so well. My students' favorite station was the one where they had tea time and learned about manners.
>
> —Mrs. Whitlow, English teacher

Other

There are other tools that can be applied at various learning stations. Google Earth, for example, is fantastic and can be applicable to all subject areas. Providing aerial views of urban, suburban, and rural areas captured from Google Earth drives students' understanding of the differences between these three types of living environments. Students can also navigate through Google Earth to determine the elevation of the top and bottom of a ski slope and to figure out the distance from the beginning of the ski slope to the end, in order to calculate its slope. Manipulating its historical imagery function allows students to see the effects of erosion on the California coastline, or the effects of gentrification in Harlem. Google Earth has many excellent uses, is real-world based, and is something students enjoy.

Giant timelines are creative tools for students to manipulate in order to display what they are learning, but also to understand the causal relationship of events. This method gets students to think critically when researching immigration. The immigrants that came to the United States when they did came here because things were pushing them out of their home countries and/or pulling them toward the United States. Students can place world events on a giant timeline and notice that several million Irish came to the United States during and after the Irish Potato Famine, which wiped out their main source of food. They can see the years that immigrants were coming over in droves, because the Homestead Act passed and the Transcontinental Railroad was being built, giving poor people an opportunity to have land and a job. This type of learning station is most successful when a librarian or teacher facilitates the discussion in Socratic style. (See Immigration Learning Stations)

Timeline of world events affecting or effected by immigration

Reading and interpreting charts is difficult for most students. Many great charts and infographics can be found online for use in multimedia learning stations. Students can practice gathering information from bar graphs, pie charts, flow charts, Venn Diagrams, and infographics. Because of the difficulty students tend to have comprehending graphs and charts, it is recommended that the librarian or teacher provide guidance. Charts can also be created by students to display what they learn. A Venn diagram is a visual students that can complete with the research they collect to show their understanding. It helps show the relationships between two or more things by exploring their similarities and differences.

Citation Makers

Citation makers are invaluable during multimedia learning stations. Citing sources is one of the necessary skills librarians teach students and one that students need to continue practicing throughout school. EasyBib (http://www.easybib.com/) and Citation Machine (http://www.citationmachine.net/) are both good websites that students navigate through fairly easily to create a citation. EasyBib even has a research tool within it that students can explore when researching, which tells students whether or not the source is deemed to be credible. Citing all of the sources contained within a set of multimedia learning stations isn't necessary, because many of the sources are provided for them. When creating a citation does apply, though, students have an invaluable opportunity to practice citing.

Bringing It All Together

There are many different ways to construct a set of multimedia learning stations. Stronger sets of learning stations employ different resources and opportunities for group and individual work at each learning station. When creating learning stations, the sources, topics, and information that students will be exploring should be diversified. Diversity will make the learning stations more interesting, more memorable, and more fun.

4

When and How to Use Multimedia Learning Stations

Group or Individual Work

Some learning stations are most successful when students are working independently, while others benefit from collaborative group work. When groups collaborate, they often help each other if there is confusion. It is necessary to offer both independent and collaborative activities throughout a set of multimedia learning stations, so that students learn to work both together and independently. Thought processes are different in both types of groupings. Students can often expand their understanding of a topic by building upon one another, but they also need to practice learning and thinking critically on their own.

> You get to work in groups when in stations.
>
> —Travon, student

> Stations are easier to do together, rather than learning alone.
>
> —Marvin, student

Take multimedia learning stations on the Vietnam War, for example. The standards for the Vietnam War should be downloaded from the state Department of Education website. The classroom teacher and the librarian should decide upon which standards to specifically target and then begin searching for sources students should use to research each of these topics. Once the standards are matched with the sources of material that were found, the topics and sources can be chosen, based upon what is best suited for independent work or for group work. Due to the nature of how videos and podcasts are used for research, those learning stations generally employ independent work, because they don't provide as much opportunity for discussion during the research process.

An example of a set of multimedia learning stations could be laid out as follows:

Topic: The Vietnam War

Station 1: Vietnam: The Country and Its History - Books, eBooks, and Encyclopedias - collaborative groups

Station 2: Frontlines of the War - Websites - collaborative groups

Station 3: The Anti-War Movement - Videos, Pictures, and Music - independent work

Station 4: Media Coverage of the War - Videos of Primary Source News Broadcasts - independent work

Station 5: Memorials and War Veterans - Podcasts - independent work

Station 6: Statistics and Information - Databases - collaborative groups

After these decisions have been made, questions are created to go with each source. Addressing many levels of Bloom's Taxonomy should be a goal (Bloom, 1956), (Anderson & Krathwohl, 2001). To help address this goal, a Bloom's Taxonomy Question Wheel can be used. There are many of these wheels on the market, and some are even available for free online.

Chapter 5 of this book goes into more detail about quality questioning and Bloom's Taxonomy Question Wheels. These wheels can be invaluable when creating learning stations, because they ensure that students will not only be locating and accessing information, but that they will be thinking critically about the information they are finding.

When Can Multimedia Learning Stations Be Used?

When used for curricular purposes, the format and structure of learning stations can be effective as an introduction to a unit, a part of an overall unit, a review, a culminating activity, or an extension activity. Regardless of when information is used, students learn to locate and access information of all types, analyze it, and react or reflect upon it. Learning stations can be used in isolation, or they can be used to gather research that students will utilize for a larger project. The overall purpose of the learning station activity will dictate its design.

Introduction

When learning stations are used as an introduction to a unit, they often center on locating and accessing information rather than having students thinking critically about it. It is difficult for students to react to a situation they haven't learned about. If a student doesn't know who the first five U.S. presidents were and what their policies were, it is hard for them to compare and contrast their presidencies. Students would need to research sources during multimedia learning stations to gather information for later use.

Locating and accessing information using school subscription databases

In an example set of multimedia learning stations on the first five presidents, students find information on the presidents from the White House government website, details about their homes from the respective presidential home websites and included videos, and specifics about their early lives from the school subscription databases. Students make presidential trading cards as study tools for later. These types of learning stations provide students with a foundation of information to expand and reflect upon later in the classroom. (See First Five Presidents Learning Stations)

Middle of Unit

My students have enjoyed completing many different stations in the library. They have been able to learn detailed background knowledge necessary for helping them to get the most out of novel studies. They have completed stations centered around the Great Depression while reading *Roll of Thunder, Hear My Cry*. They have researched disabilities and the setting of the story while reading *Freak the Mighty*. My students have gained knowledge of the different types of poetry through poetry stations created by Mrs. Spisak. My students have been exposed to topics they wouldn't have otherwise been exposed to.

— Danielle Sommers, reading teacher

Multimedia learning stations can also be used in the middle of a unit of study. They can build upon what was already learned in the classroom, and they can introduce students to things that are coming next. This situation provides a great opportunity to employ educational apps for portable devices. These apps can be found in the iTunes store for Apple devices such as iPads, iPods, and iPhones. They can also be found on Google Play or at the Amazon Appstore, for Android devices. If there are portable devices in a library, they can be used for multimedia learning stations. If not, it may be a good opportunity to try BYOD (Bring Your Own Device) for the day. Many of these apps are free and easy to download, and would accommodate two or three students sharing a device to navigate the app.

An example of a set of learning stations used in the middle of a unit of study can be found in the cells learning stations. Students are expected to have already learned a little bit about plant and animal cells in the classroom. Building on this knowledge, students are asked to use the iCell app from Apple's App Store to review and expand their understanding of the differences between the two. iCell is a free app that shows magnified plant and animal cells.

Students can enlarge them, manipulate them, and discover more information about them as they go. They simply tap to open information on each of the parts of the cells. This process allows students to readily see and understand the differences between the two types of cells. Also included in this set of learning stations, are instructions for searching the subscription databases to explore bacteria, video streaming services to explore fungi, microviewers and pamphlets for protists, and a video from the National Geographic website on viruses. (See Cells Learning Stations)

Test Review

My civics classes loved the citizenship stations, and especially the music that played during the transition times. Their completed packets are perfect for review before the SOL [Standards of Learning] test in June.

— Mrs. Bolling, history teacher

Multimedia learning stations can be used for review before a unit test. In these types of learning stations, all the necessary standards can be targeted, and the material can be reviewed in new ways. In multimedia learning stations on fractions, students look up information in the school subscription databases and then play games to practice them. They use math books (not textbooks) found on the library bookshelves to solve mysteries, a student-created rap video on TeacherTube that reminds them how to simplify fractions, and a database or a website to find a recipe and determine how to add amounts of ingredients in the recipe, and to see what size bowl they should use to mix the ingredients.

Students are also provided with a variety of high-interest nonfiction books to choose from. Once they select a book, they convert its Dewey Decimal Number into a "Dewey Fraction Number." Any time that books can be put on a table to expose students to them, it's a good thing. Inevitably something from the selected sources will be checked out at the end of class. By the end of the learning stations activity, students have practiced everything they needed for their test, and they did so with a different format that taught them valuable skills needed for searching databases and TeacherTube. (See Fractions Learning Stations)

Culminating Activity

Multimedia learning stations for the 1955 play *The Diary of Anne Frank* were designed as a culminating activity. Students needed to finish reading the play before using these learning stations, so that they would already know of Anne Frank's death and the survival of her father. In these learning stations, students could reach beyond the play, exploring what happened after the play ends.

They learned about concentration camps from websites, read an interview conducted with one of the protectors of the Franks, Miep Gies, watched a primary source interview with Otto Frank from the 1980s, explored pictures of the secret annex from the website for the Anne Frank House, learned about Hitler and the Hitler Youth by watching a primary source video from the United States Holocaust Memorial Museum of Hitler speaking at a youth rally, read testimonials from children who experienced the Holocaust, and listened to a primary source radio broadcast from the day a concentration camp was liberated.

Watching and listening to Holocaust survivor testimony

These multimedia learning stations not only enhanced students' knowledge of the Holocaust and increased their compassion for Anne Frank and all Holocaust victims, but they also taught them to question and stand up for things. Even though these learning stations contain opportunities

> My classes participated in stations for a research unit about medieval life. We had just finished reading historical fiction set in the time period, and it was enlightening for students to delve into the realities of life in an ancient time! They loved the websites of course, but the books that were sitting at some stations captured some children's attention and they asked to borrow the books just for fun after we finished our unit! This is one of the best methods to reinforce learning that I have used! Thanks for your hard work in preparing the stations!
>
> — Mrs. Loan, English teacher

for both group and independent work, the mood of the room during them is silent and powerful. (See Anne Frank Learning Stations)

Occasionally after a unit of study, teachers want their students to explore a topic beyond what they learned in the classroom. Sometimes subject standards don't cover all of the connections a teacher wants to make, between what a student is learning and how the topic affects people and the world. Sometimes student understanding isn't fully reached through the standards. The World War II historical novel *Milkweed* by Jerry Spinelli can be taught at the same time history classes teach World War II. Through this cross-curricular unit, students learn about Jewish ghettos, the Holocaust, Hitler, and concentration camps in their history classes, as they read about well-developed characters trying to survive in the Warsaw Ghetto.

In order to broaden students' experience with the novel, a set of multimedia learning stations could extend the lesson beyond the English and history standards. In the first learning station, students

Viewing images of children in the Warsaw Ghetto during World War II

use an atlas to calculate the distance between Warsaw, Poland and Berlin, Germany. The atlas also helps them determine the same unit of distance between the city they live in and another major city in the United States. Comparing the two distances helps students make the connection about the proximity of the original two cities. They don't usually visualize Berlin and Warsaw being so close to each other.

Students also research children of the Warsaw Ghetto on the United States Holocaust Memorial Museum website, and in books and eBooks from the library collection. Students' use of primary source pictures of the children of the Warsaw Ghetto connects them to the unimaginable environment that is the setting of the novel they are reading.

Students also watch video testimonials of survivors of the Warsaw Ghetto, and as a class, watch and discuss primary source footage of the Warsaw Ghetto Uprising. This experience provides an opportunity to discuss the differences between a primary source and a secondary source. It also can spark a discussion about the difference between real, primary-source footage, and the fictionalized accounts that students see in the movie theater.

In addition to these learning stations, students search the databases and books to research the real-life people who appear in the novel, and the diseases that spread throughout the ghettos. They are able to analyze the information they find on typhus and tuberculosis, to determine why these diseases ran rampant through the ghettos and concentration camps. (See *Milkweed* Learning Stations)

Big Research Project

Gathering research to help with an overall project is another way to implement multimedia learning stations. An example of this method is in a set of learning stations on biomes. During these multimedia learning stations, students are asked to research and get an overview of six major biomes specified in their content standards. They then choose one of the biomes from the research they gathered during this set of learning stations as their topic for a larger project.

There are six different learning stations in this set, one for each biome. Students rotate through the first five learning stations, using a different source at each one. The learning station sources consist of school subscription databases, Google Advanced Search, books and eBooks, print and electronic encyclopedias, and preselected websites compiled on the tool ThingLink (https://www.thinglink.com/).

The sixth and final learning station has all students researching the same biome, but each student chooses, of the previous five learning stations of research resources, which learning station to return to. Individual students choose the learning station that applied the research method they would like to use again to research the final biome, and they return to it.

The next class period, in the classroom, students can choose the biome that interested them the most to be the topic of a larger research project. They can choose partners, use the information they gathered, and go back to gather more information as needed from the types of research sources they learned in the library. Since creating citations was built into this set of learning stations, students are able to have a completed Works Cited page at the end of their project. For younger students or novices to citations, the citation component may need to be addressed in a separate lesson due, to the time constraints involved. (See Biomes Learning Stations.)

The biomes set of multimedia learning stations is also an example of teaching students about multiple types of resources through guided practice. This guided research sets them up for selecting one of the resources on their own for the last learning station. They practice using all of them, then select one on their own in the end. This independent choice sets students up to be more prepared to select research sources on their own in future. They are provided with research skills, and are able to begin establishing a more solid research process.

5

Quality Questioning

Quality design of multimedia learning stations depends on three things: good resources, organization, and quality questioning. Students need to not only find facts, but to also think about those facts, create new knowledge, make connections to the real world, share those facts with others, and grow from the experience. These things may not all happen in one learning station, and they may not all happen in one particular set of learning stations, but it is important to scaffold toward those goals.

Most learning stations have thinking questions attached to them. Even learning stations that ask students to collect facts generally have a thinking or discussion question to go with them. It is important for students to show evidence that they are thinking about what they learn, beyond the facts they are asked to find.

A lot of research has been conducted on how to create questions of quality. Questioning using the levels of Bloom's Taxonomy increases the authentic learning that allows students to grow as individuals, thinkers, and citizens.

Bloom's Taxonomy Questions

Bloom's Taxonomy was published in 1956, in the book *Taxonomy of Educational Objectives: The Classification of Educational Goals, Handbook 1: Cognitive Domain*. Designed to classify goals for education, the work was created by a team of educators and edited by Benjamin Bloom.

Bloom's Taxonomy was successful because it was a strong tool for evaluating objectives, and it allowed for detailed goals. This way of assessing had not been done before (Marzano, 2007). The process broke thinking and ways of evaluating student learning into six groups:

- **Knowledge** - information retrieval; remembering what was learned

- **Comprehension** - knowing what is being communicated, and being able to understand and make use of it

- **Application** - being able to use what was learned without assistance

- **Analysis** - being able to determine the relationships between what was learned and other things

- **Synthesis** - creating new knowledge based on what was learned

- **Evaluation** - assessing knowledge that was either self- or teacher-generated

Bloom and the other authors of *Taxonomy of Educational Objectives* admit that evaluation may not always be the last step. Evaluation is placed last on their scale because, in order to occur, it relies on the other components within the scale. However, creative and critical thinking and the development of new knowledge can also occur after evaluation has taken place (Bloom, 1956).

In 2001 Lorin W. Anderson and David R. Krathwohl published an updated version of Bloom's Taxonomy, in *A Taxonomy for Learning, Teaching, and Assessing: A Revision of Bloom's Taxonomy of Educational Objectives*. Much of the original structure stays the same, but terminology and some ordering of the levels of the taxonomy differ from the original. Anderson and Krathwohl present the following restructured version of Bloom's Taxonomy (Anderson, 2001):

- **Remembering** - being able to recall

- **Understanding** - making meaning from learning

- **Applying** - being able to complete a task with learned information

- **Analyzing** - figuring out how things relate to each other

- **Evaluating** - assessing learning based on standards and objectives

- **Creating** - creating new knowledge from learned information

Based on the new Bloom's Taxonomy, each example set of multimedia learning stations presented in Part Two of this book contains a section that identifies the highest level of questioning involved at each respective learning station. Multiple levels of questioning may occur in each learning station from "remembering" to "creating," with the highest level indicated.

> My sixth graders loved going to the library for the fractions stations. Not only were they learning about fraction concepts and operations, they were exposed to fractions in literature, real-world applications, and 21st-century skills. Mrs. Spisak really makes sure that all of her stations are at the higher end of Bloom's Taxonomy. I wish there was time to do more.
>
> — Allison Feinmel, math teacher

Bloom's Taxonomy Question Wheel

A valuable tool to have when creating questions for multimedia learning stations, is a question wheel based on Bloom's Taxonomy. The question-starters that these wheels provide are invaluable. They help the librarian build quality questions that address all levels of Bloom's Taxonomy.

Many companies make these wheels, and others can be found online for free. A benefit of purchasing one through a company is that it usually results in a very sturdy wheel that provides questions for each level. Some purchased versions of the wheel even provide extra information such as action words or an explanation of the levels of Bloom's Taxonomy. The company Mentoring Minds (https://www.mentoringminds.com/) has very good question wheels that offer a lot of information and hold up well over time.

Thinking within Multimedia Learning Stations

A set of discussion questions or individual thought-provoking questions can be asked, in order to increase the level of thinking and exploration students do at a learning station. The questions created for each learning station should not only address the overall purpose of what students are learning, but also encourage students to explore ideas that can stem from the initial learning and, possibly, create a new context for it.

> It's a great way to exercise our brains.
>
> —DJ, student

Steps for Questions

Quality questions need to be created thoughtfully. Following are the four most important steps to take when creating questions for multimedia learning stations:

1. Identify purpose based on standards, objectives, and essential questions

2. Determine cognitive ability of students

3. Form questions that address what students should learn

4. When appropriate, create a discussion idea or a thought-provoking question or series of questions

Identifying the purpose of the lesson should be done in collaboration with the classroom teacher using the state or national standards, and any state or district curriculum frameworks. The goal of the librarian is to infuse the required standards-based core curriculum with the AASL's standards for the 21st-century learner. This task should be done with the classroom teacher to ensure that the content purpose is correct, and so that the teacher can see the deliberate thinking of the librarian, in addition to the sincere desire to collaborate.

Establishing the cognitive ability of students is important. The intent isn't to determine who should have higher level questions, but to determine how much scaffolding needs to occur to get to the higher level questions. Although teachers often assume lower ability learners and special education students cannot answer questions that ask for higher level thinking, studies show that they can: thinking at a higher level is something all students are capable of when they are trained in how to do so (Walsh and Sattes, 2008).

When creating questions that address the specific content students need to learn, a librarian should strive to be clear and concise. It can help to have a person other than the librarian and content teacher involved in the lesson to read over questions for clarity. Because students are responsible for knowing specific content as well as thinking about the information they are learning, it is necessary to have questions addressing varying levels of Bloom's Taxonomy. Questions on the "remembering" level are important, in order for students to gather the information they

Students gather information to respond to higher level questions

need to learn. Students need to gather the information before they can move to higher levels on the scale.

Kathy Schrock has an alternative and intriguing way of visualizing the levels of Bloom's Taxonomy. She sees them not as a pyramid of scaled importance, but rather as a set of interlocking gears. Each level is important, and students may find themselves moving in and out of each of the various types of questioning as they raise their levels of thinking (Schrock, 2011). She also has files listed on her website (http://www.schrockguide.net/bloomin-apps.html) for making posters for the library or classroom, as well as lists of various apps that can be used on iOS or Android devices that will address each level of Bloom's Taxonomy.

Many topics lend themselves to discussion questions for a group. Other topics with more content-specific means may be better served by having students gather information in some questions and then respond to a thought-provoking question that gets them to extend their thinking about the information in a different way. It is necessary for the librarian and teacher to determine how they want the questions to work. "Gather and discuss" or "gather and think" tends to be the most common method of questioning in most subject- and standards-based multimedia learning stations.

Socratic Spurts

Librarians and teachers can lead discussion to explore thinking. Socratic Spurts are based on the idea of a Socratic Seminar, but in a much shorter form. The Socratic method involves a facilitator asking open-ended questions to a group that is charged with discussing the questions using evidence from a text (Israel, 2002). Exploring text or information in this way prompts students to think further and determine what happened, why it happened, and/or where the topic may go in the future. Socratic Spurts are intended to be discussed in a few short minutes, rather than in lengthy discussions.

In an example set of multimedia learning stations on immigration, students explore Google Earth aerial images that depict a rural, an urban, and a suburban community. In exploring these images, students are asked, "Why would immigrants in the early 1900s have started moving out of the rural areas and into urban areas?" Expanding on this idea of an increased population in cities, students discuss ideas stemming from the question, "What type of buildings might have been invented during this time, to house the large numbers of people moving to the cities?"

At another learning station in the set, students have a giant timeline with specific world events listed. Exploring what was happening in the world during the specific years given, students are able to determine through discussion what was pulling immigrants from specific countries to the United States at that time, and to also see what factors were pushing people out of their home countries and to the United States. (See Immigration Learning Stations)

Using a timeline, students make connections between the causes and effects of immigration

Images from Google Earth of local urban, suburban, and rural areas

A group participating in a Socratic Spurt with their history teacher

Mini-Discussions

Teachers can begin a discussion after first giving students a chance to think about a question, then asking them to write down their initial thoughts (Walsh and Sattes, 2008). This mini-discussion can be facilitated by the librarian or the teacher. Enough time should be built in for this discussion to occur. The discussion may be the main emphasis of the particular learning station where it occurs, or it may be a shorter piece of closure to end the learning station.

Small Group to Large Group Discussion

Another option for including facilitative discussion would be to establish the last learning station of a set as being the point at which students come together with their individual groups, to discuss one or two of the essential questions from the day and explore them further. Each student has something to contribute, and he or she should be given an opportunity to write down thoughts, communicate and collaborate with their group, and then come together for a larger group discussion.

> It gives you a chance to work alone and with a group.
> — Kennedy, student

This type of discussion can be conducted face-to-face as a whole group or in an online discussion forum. An online discussion forum has the advantage of allowing more opportunity for each student to contribute thoughts without having to speak in front of a group. It would be a mandate of the online discussion forum that each student would have to make a contribution.

Summary

Quality questions are an important means for students to gather facts, think about them, and to be able to use them in other contexts. Questions can be presented for each level of Bloom's Taxonomy and can be answered individually as part of the discussion at a learning station, or in an online discussion forum. Students need to be trained, and to have proper scaffolding built into the climate of a classroom and/or in a set of multimedia learning stations. Students of all ability levels are able to answer higher-level thinking questions when they have been trained to do so. Although not all sets of multimedia learning stations require questions at each level of Bloom's Taxonomy, students should be able to show evidence of having learned facts and of knowing how to think beyond them.

> Stations give you more than one way to learn a topic.
> — Summer, student

6

Rotation and Time Limits

Students' movement to and accomplishment of each learning station can be orchestrated in a variety of ways. Learning stations can be designed for students to rotate to after a set amount of time, at their own pace, or to learning stations of their choosing, when presented with a variety from which to choose. Learning stations can be designed to be completed in one class period in the library, or over two class periods that begin in the library and end in the classroom. Occasionally, depending on time and the length of the learning stations, the librarian can set up duplicate versions of the learning stations to minimize the number of students in a given place at the same time. Librarians and teachers have a lot of flexibility deciding how students move from one learning station to the next.

Timed Learning Stations

Students tend to work best if they are given a set amount of time at each learning station. Often they need the push of a time limit to get them moving and motivate them to finish. A set of learning stations on the Harlem Renaissance provides such time limits. These learning stations cover the key figures of the time period, including Jacob Lawrence, Langston Hughes, Duke Ellington, Bessie Smith, and Louis Armstrong. They also cover important places and popular nightlife such as the Apollo Theatre, the Cotton Club, and house rent parties. Students learn about the history of Harlem and its renaissance, as well as the advent of jazz and the inception of the Jazz Age.

Students have just enough time to experience the flavor of each of these people, places, and occurrences, using music, videos, databases, and websites such as Jacob Lawrence's official webpage

Stations are a great way for students to learn new content or do more in-depth study of content they already know. The limited amount of time at each station helps to keep the learners on track and keeps them from getting bored. My students love to have the chance to get up and move to a new seat after about 10 minutes at a station. Stations also are a great way to differentiate instruction, in that the learners work until they are out of time, and there is no pressure if one child does not answer as many questions as another. Stations also promote collaborative learning, in that those in the same group work together to find answers.

——Caryn Boehm, special education English and history teacher

A running online egg timer shown on an LCD screen can keep students constantly aware of how much time they have left at a learning station.

Many sets of multimedia learning stations include some stations that students can finish quickly, but others take more time. The librarian should prepare to give students information before the lesson about what to do if they finish a learning station early. If a student or group finishes one early, they should begin on the next one, even if it isn't yet time to rotate. They may also use the extra time to complete a previous learning station they had left incomplete. If the students do not finish a learning station by the time they need to rotate, they should remember to go back and complete it, if they finish another with time to spare. The librarian can post signs serving as reminders of such, at the specific learning stations that students tend to finish quickly.

Transition time during stations is eagerly awaited by my students, because when the timer rings, and the 80s rock music starts, students know that it's time to move to the next station and begin work. This allows for the movement from station to station, without breaking the flow of the lesson.

——Kathy Richardson, science teacher

and the Library of Congress. When it is time to rotate from one learning station to the next, the sounds of Ellington, Armstrong, and Smith fill the library. Incorporating music that fits the topic is always a good idea. Music becomes the cue for students to rotate. They condition to it well, and it is much more pleasant than shouting "Rotate!" or sounding a buzzer or kitchen timer. Plus, the music is part of the culture and part of the experience of what they are learning. Through it they are able to feel what they are researching. (See Harlem Renaissance Learning Stations)

Untimed Learning Stations

Sometimes the librarian and the teacher determine that students would be better served by an untimed set of learning stations. High-level learners as well as low-level learners do not always perform as well as others in timed sessions at learning stations. These students tend to work better at their own paces. They may not stay at one learning station the whole time; however, they shouldn't be pressured to move before they are ready, nor should they be held back by their peers if they are ready to move on.

When students rotate at their own pace, the librarian and teacher need to be diligent in making sure students are neither spending too much time at any one learning station, nor rushing through answers that require more thoughtful responses in order to "get it all done." It's a delicate balance, and one that needs to be constantly managed.

Algebra students' exploration of slope through multimedia learning stations illustrates such independent pacing. In this set of learning stations, students can move at very different paces. Students collaborating with a partner or a group of three works best for this set. Students watch a video clip from TeacherTube called "Slope Dude" and then apply their knowledge of slope to identify positive, negative, zero, and undefined slope on a model roller coaster. The roller coaster should be made ahead of time with the K'NEX construction system.

At the second learning station, students watch a "Steepness" video in a subscription video streaming service, a YouTube video, or a DVD from the library. Next, students go onto Google Earth to look for a ski slope in one of the ski resorts near where they live. The librarian can give them a list of resorts that are close by to search. Using this location in Google Earth, students measure the elevation at the top and bottom of the ski slope, then measure the distance between them, to calculate the slope's steepness and slope value.

In the third learning station, students download a best practices road manual to look at the maximum grade (slope) allowed for a log truck road. They apply this information with the math they have learned in the classroom, to see if a (previously built) model road meets the criteria set forth in the road manual. Once students figure out it is too steep, they need to recalculate what the heighth of the model should be, assuming the length stays the same.

Finally, in the fourth learning station, students research *lines* and *slope* in the subscription databases, and practice calculating slope-intercept form, using giant coordinate planes, Play-Doh, and string (See Slope Learning Stations).

> Models, using K'NEX or other materials, can be built ahead of time during Makerspaces sessions with students.

> Jen provides rich learning experiences, where students are learning about challenging math concepts without even knowing it. She even built a roller coaster to help the students explore the concept of slope and linear equations!
>
> —Lauren Gilkey, math teacher

A roller coaster built to help algebra classes explore slope

A model road for students to use in conjunction with an online best practices road manual for logging roads

Library to Classroom

Often, teachers and librarians want to cover more topics than they can fit into one class period. Since scheduling two class periods in the library is often difficult when the library schedule is full, the lesson can be split between the library and the classroom. The first day is spent with the librarian in the library. On the second day, the teacher takes the materials for the learning stations into the classroom, and completes the second half. This combination works well when more than one class period is required to cover the desired content.

The Outsiders by S. E. Hinton is read in English classes all over the country every year. Even 50 years after its publication, it remains relevant, and touches many students in a way other books have not been able to. The book offers more topics to cover and more connections to be made than students can be expected to condense into one class period. The rigid dichotomy between the classes in *The Outsiders* and those of the present day presents a plethora of topics, but since the novel's cultural references are from 1960s, students have a hard time understanding them.

Again, music is a key component of these learning stations. The Beatles, Elvis Presley, and Bob Dylan are all mentioned as musical artists the characters in *The Outsiders* enjoy. Introducing students to who these artists are, then having students research the artists' careers on the Rock and Roll Hall of Fame website, opens doors of understanding. Students can also research the difference between Corvair and Mustang car models, by viewing images and reading about the features of these cars using car websites. This process gives the students an entirely new understanding of those opposites. In another learning station, students research gangs, family violence, and teen runaways in today's culture, and make connections between the lives of the kids in *The Outsiders* and those of themselves and their peers. Students look at types of prejudice, compare them, and ultimately understand that it is classism, not racism, which causes the rifts between the two groups of characters in the book.

Students look at pictures and video clips of Paul Newman from the 1960s to see why Ponyboy idolizes the actor, who portrayed the tough guy in the movies. They look at how the number of drive-in movie theaters has declined over the last 50 years, and how many, if any, remain standing in the areas where they live. In another learning station, S. E. Hinton conducts a video interview (albeit from 1995), where students learn that she's female and was 16 years old when she wrote *The Outsiders*. That is a revelation to them, and opens a door of possibility that wasn't present before. Obviously, students can discover countless connections in *The Outsiders*; therefore, rushing these students through the learning stations in one 90-minute class period would do neither them nor the novel justice (See *Outsiders* Learning Stations).

Duplicate Sets

Searching for online images of Paul Newman for learning stations on *The Outsiders* by S. E. Hinton

If a large amount of time is required to complete individual multimedia learning stations, more than one set should be prepared. Having a duplicate set means fewer learning stations with fewer students. Sometimes, due to the amount of content and the application of knowledge students are required to put forth at each learning station, it is advantageous to keep the number of learning stations to three or four instead of five or six. This setup gives students more time for students to spend at each learning station. However, in order to avoid groups with excessive numbers of students in them, it is imperative that multiple sets of the same learning stations be created.

When conducting multimedia learning stations on surface area and volume with math classes, the librarian should provide two duplicate sets of three learning stations. Students need extra time to complete the calculations involved in these learning stations, and having only three stops to make requires less rotation and, consequently, provides more time at each learning station. At one station, students watch two video clips from a subscription video streaming service. One of the clips addresses the surface area of the Great Pyramid, and the other addresses the volume of water in pools. Students may complete this learning station individually with headphones, or they may watch the videos together as they play from one source.

In the next learning station, an interactive website walks them through how to calculate surface area and volume. It shows them clips of how 3D shapes unroll into 2D shapes, and it helps them calculate the surface area and volume of each shape.

The third learning station shows them a 3D image of what happens to the surface area and volume of an object when the width, length, and heighth of a rectangle are adjusted. This image helps students visualize a concept that is very abstract. Following the third station, students calculate the surface area of 2D paper images (NETS), then fold them into 3D prisms, which are displayed in the library.

Although no databases are required in this set of learning stations, students are directed to reliable math websites, as well as a subscription video streaming service (See Surface Area and Volume Learning Stations).

Student Choice

At times, usually for enrichment or extension activity learning stations, the librarian can offer students a variety of learning stations, and the students choose which they will go to. This type of set of multimedia learning stations is employed if a teacher feels students are getting the curricular standards they need in the classroom, but would like students to make more connections between the subject matter and the real world.

A good example of student-choice multimedia learning stations would be one that focuses on rocks and minerals for Earth science students. Nine real-world-based learning stations about rocks and minerals are available for students. Students choose any four of the nine they would like to explore. The topics range from diamond mining to mineral makeup to farming to the exchange rate of gold, silver, and copper. Since many learning stations are available to choose from, students often say this set of learning stations is their all-time favorite. Also, because they are only required to choose four of nine learning stations, they don't feel rushed, and are able to fully explore their interests (See Rocks and Minerals Learning Stations).

Using a reliable website as a research resource during the "Student Choice" learning station

Closing

Students can rotate through sets of multimedia learning stations in many ways. Librarians should thoughtfully consider the number of learning stations, the number of sets of learning stations, and the amount of content within each learning station. The academic level of students should be factored in as well. Finally, the librarian and teacher should monitor the progress of students as they are researching, encourage them, and offer time-management suggestions along the way.

7

Assessment

For multimedia learning stations, student self-assessment strategies can help ascertain what each student has learned, and what needs to be improved in a lesson. Teachers are often the primary decision makers on how to assess the final product for a set of multimedia learning stations in their classrooms, but assessment can also be collaborative with the librarian, incorporating the AASL standards within the general assessment. The librarian can also include other types of assessment that go beyond the final product assessment. These types of assessment can be completed in the library at the end of the class period, to help determine progress and growth.

Assessment can provide a way not only to gauge a student's learning and improve on the lesson for next time, but also to provide data to help support the library program. This data can be used to show other teachers, specialists, and administrators how the library program is making a difference, by showing how it impacts student achievement. A good way to gather this data is to have students complete a self-assessment both before and after their multimedia learning station experience.

Good self-assessments include subject content questions, as well as research process questions. Including the same questions on both the pre- and post-self-assessments allows data to be collected that shows student growth.

Types of Assessment

According to Violet H. Harada and Joan M. Yoshina in *Assessing for Learning*, assessment is the process of analyzing and reporting on collected data that informs students and teachers where students are successful and where they are struggling (Harada & Yoshina, 2010). There are three types of assessment: summative, formative, and metacognitive.

Summative assessment evaluates learning for evidence of achievement. This is generally conducted at the end of a unit, and compares the work against a standard or a set learning goal. Examples of summative assessments are tests, exams, and term papers (Formative vs Summative Assessment, n.d.).

Formative assessment, instead of evaluating final performance, assesses ongoing or daily student progress, and how students are learning (Harada & Yoshina, 2010). Formative assessment relies on constant feedback between teacher and student, and should not have a formal grade attached to it. Some examples of formative assessments are exit tickets or daily conferences.

Metacognitive assessment centers on student reflection, self-assessment, and using feedback to improve future process and performance (Zmuda, 2010). Allison Zmuda argues in *Breaking Free from Myths About Teaching and Learning* that metacognitive assessment must occur in order for successful learning to occur. She also states the need for this type of assessment to be explicitly taught to students because it is not an intuitive skill. Examples of metacognitive assessments include self-assessments conducted throughout class, and at the end of class.

Assessment for Multimedia Learning Stations

All three forms of assessment are applicable when using multimedia learning stations. The summative assessment is but a small part of the overall assessment. In conducting pre- and post-assessments, summative data is collected comparing what students know about the content before and what they know after. This type of data is important in showing the efficacy of multimedia learning stations, and the library program as a whole, in increasing student achievement. The data collected does not have to be used as a grade. Some teachers may choose to use the accuracy of student answers on the learning stations document as a formal grade, but most do not. Most choose an alternate form of summative assessment. More will be mentioned on that in a later section of this chapter.

Multimedia learning stations authentically embed formative assessment. During these learning stations, the librarian and the teacher conduct ongoing formative assessments, facilitating the instruction and the learning as it occurs in the library. They are constantly observing and providing feedback to groups and individual students to help when they show signs of struggle and, equally important, when things are going well. This combination of a facilitative teaching approach and ongoing formative assessment makes learning stations successful in building skills and establishing dispositions and responsibilities in students.

Because of the focus on the AASL standards, both formative and metacognitive assessments are the preferred methods of assessment for the librarian using multimedia learning stations. Metacognitive assessment occurs at the end of a learning stations activity, when students conduct the post self-assessment. In addition to content questions, students are asked to reflect on the research process, what they would do differently or the same in the future, and why they would choose that course of action. This self-reflective process informs the librarian about whether or not process learning is occurring. It reveals whether skills are truly being built and if dispositions and responsibilities are actually being established.

Assessment *for* Learning

In focusing more on the formative and metacognitive assessments, and less on the summative, assessment *for* learning occurs, rather than assessment *of* learning. When assessing *for* learning, partnerships are built between students, teachers, and librarians. Because there is both a shift from grades to learning and a constant flow of information between the students, teachers, and librarians, the stress a student may feel about performance is alleviated, allowing more dialogue and genuine understanding to occur. Students begin to see and understand what success looks like.

Student self-assessments focus on the learning process. They enable students to become more responsible for their own learning, evaluate themselves in multiple ways, reflect on their process to determine what made them successful (or not), and decide what they can do to improve their work. The responsibility for improving their process for future research lies with the student. Self-assessment gives students ownership of their own learning.

Tools to Use for Self-Assessment

A variety of instruments can be used for self-assessments. Checklists and rubrics provide a qualitative glimpse into how a student feels they are progressing. Exit tickets allow students to self-assess their process, as well display summative content knowledge. Anecdotal reflections and paragraphs, or self-made lists of what was learned, provide opportunities for more reflection and thought about the learning and research process, while online forms or surveys provide quantitative data, as well as opportunities to reflect on personal learning and process.

Checklists and Rubrics

Checklists contain a list of content information and research processes students should have mastered by the end of a set of learning stations. Students can check off an item once they feel it has been mastered or successfully learned.

Rubrics, while appearing to be similar, are actually quite different. Rubrics make use of a chart layout to list the criteria for what makes student work meet, exceed, or fall below expectations. These types of rubrics can be limiting at times, but a single-point rubric is more expansive. The single-point rubric combines the list of a checklist with a chart that helps students determine where they are going, where they are, what they still need to do, and how they will go beyond the requirements (Fluckiger, 2012).

Another type of single-point rubric details the requirements for an assignment in the center column, while the columns to the left and right are blank, and allow a teacher to provide feedback. This feedback details the specifics of what caused an assignment to not meet expectations, as well elaborate on the elements that exceeded expectations (Gonzalez, 2014). For examples, see Figure 7.1 for a checklist, Figure 7.2 for a rubric, and Figure 7.3 for a single-point rubric.

FIGURE 7.1   Checklist Rubric Example

Probability, Percents, Ratios and Proportions Learning Stations Student Checklist

Goal to Accomplish	Yes, I've Accomplished It	No, I Need Help
Learn to research using multiple resources		
Determine Probability		
Figure Out Percents		
Understand Ratios and Proportions		
Be able to create a model to scale		
Try again and again when confused		

FIGURE 7.2 Multiple-Point Rubric Example

Name: _____

Math in the Library-Who Knew?!: Multimedia Stations for Probability, Percents, Ratios and Proportions

	25	20	15	10	0	SSA*	TA**
Process and Focus	Worked hard, read and followed instructions, concentrated on the task at hand, asked appropriate questions of librarian, teacher and group members when needed	Mostly worked hard, read and followed instructions, concentrated on the task at hand, asked appropriate questions of librarian, teacher and group members when needed	Minimal attempt was made to work hard, read and follow instructions, concentrate on the task at hand, ask appropriate questions of librarian, teacher and group members when needed	Rarely worked hard, read and followed instructions, concentrated on the task at hand, asked appropriate questions of librarian, teacher and group members when needed	No attempt is made	_____	_____
Teamwork/ Group work	Completely worked collaboratively with group, shared responsibility, listened, asked questions, compromised when necessary, actively contributed, discussed solutions	Mostly worked collaboratively with group, shared responsibility, listened, asked questions, compromised when necessary, actively contributed, discussed solutions	Rarely worked collaboratively with group, shared responsibility, listened, asked questions, compromised when necessary, actively contributed, discussed solutions	Worked independently and occasionally with the group	No attempt was made to work with the group	_____	_____
Accuracy of Math and Tinker Toy Scale	Accurately completed math problems and Tinker Toy scale-model	Most of work is accurate	Minimal work is accurate	Attempts math problems, but math isn't accurate	No attempt is made to complete tasks	_____	_____
Understanding	Excellent understanding of concepts explored, helps others to understand	Basic understanding of concepts	Minimal understanding of concepts	Attempts to understand concepts, but has no understanding	No attempt made to understand concepts	_____	_____

* SSA – Student Self-Assessment
** TA – Librarian/Teacher Assessment

Total _____   _____

Created by Jenifer R. Spisak
School Librarian
Hungary Creek Middle School
March 2010

FIGURE 7.3 Single-Point Rubric Example

Probability, Percents, Ratios and Proportions Learning Stations Rubric

Not Finished Yet	**Requirements**	**What Has Been Completed**	**How to Do More**
	Process		
	1. Understood research process		
	2. Used the provided sources		
	3. Tried again when confused		
	4. Understood real-world applications of probability, percents, ratios and proportions		
	Focus		
	1. Worked hard		
	2. Read and followed instructions		
	3. Concentrated on the task at hand		
	4. Asked questions of librarian, teacher and group members when needed		

(Continued)

FIGURE 7.3 Single-Point Rubric Example (*Continued*)

Probability, Percents, Ratios and Proportions Learning Stations Rubric

Not Finished Yet	Requirements	What Has Been Completed	How to Do More
	Teamwork 1. Worked collaboratively with group 2. Shared responsibility 3. Listened 4. Asked questions 5. Compromised when necessary 6. Actively contributed 7. Discussed solutions **Accuracy** 1. Correctly completed math problems 2. Accurately built Tinker Toy scale-model of skyscraper **Understanding** 1. Excellent understanding of concepts explored 2. Helped others to understand 3. Active participant in discussions		

FIGURE 7.4 Exit Ticket Example

Student Self-Assessment

Probability, Percents, Ratios and Proportions Learning Stations

Exit Ticket

Name:

1. What is something specific you learned today that you didn't know before?

2. How can probability, percents, ratios or proportions be used in real life?

3. What types of sources did you learn can be used for research purposes?

4. If you were to do these learning stations again, what would you do differently? Why?

5. Complete the following sentence. "After today I am still struggling with...

6. Complete the following sentence. "I am doing well with...

Exit Tickets

Using exit tickets is a great method for students to let the librarian and teacher know what they learned and how they feel about the learning. They have an opportunity to say what made them successful, what they would do differently, where they are still struggling, and what content they learned.

Although the content piece of the exit ticket appears to be more summative than formative, it should not be attached to a grade. Not attaching a grade to this content allows it to be a communication tool between a student and a librarian or teacher, regarding a student's progress in the exploration of the content. The teacher or librarian should follow up with feedback on areas of weakness for the exit ticket to be effective. For an example, see Figure 7.4.

Anecdotal Reflections

Students' written anecdotal reflections and paragraphs can provide librarians and teachers with great information on what students have learned. In these reflections, students talk about process and/or content. The anecdotal reflections tend to focus on one research or process question posed by the librarian.

Some possible prompts for the anecdotal reflection are:

- If you were to do these learning stations again, what would you do differently, and why?

- What research source did you struggle the most with today, and what made it difficult?

- Which of the resources that you used today do you think you will use again for future research? Explain why.

- Describe what you feel was a strength for you today. Explain why you it was a strength.

Paragraphs or lists of what students learned can inform the teacher and the librarian about the level of success students experienced during the learning stations. Students need to be taught to be specific when conveying their learning in paragraph form, and will benefit from examples of what to do versus what not to do when writing these paragraphs.

Weak Example: I learned about Duke Ellington.

Strong Example: I learned that Duke Ellington was a famous African-American bandleader during the Harlem Renaissance. His band used to play at the Cotton Club, but only white people were allowed into the club, unless they were a waiter or an entertainer.

> Anecdotal Example:
>
> If I were to do these learning stations again, I would work more as a team with my group and I would work a lot faster. I got a lot more done when we worked on learning about things instead of talking. When we talked, it was harder to concentrate. Next time I will try to focus more.
>
> — Seventh grade student

> Paragraph of Information Examples:
>
> I learned about the Cotton Club and how after it was bought by Mr. Madden that whites were the only ones that could come there as customers.
>
> I also learned that Louis Armstrong was misbehaved as a boy. He even took a gun loaded with blanks and shot at a person! For this he went to a school for misbehaved kids and learned how to play the trumpet. I was amazed that such a refined and world-renowned artist could have started out as such a terror.
>
> — Seventh grade student

Online Forms and Survey Tools

Online forms and surveys are an excellent way to assess multimedia learning stations. If students have access to computers or handheld devices, this method can provide both quantitative and qualitative data.

Many tools provide online forms and surveys that a librarian can use to gather data. Both Google Forms (https://forms.google.com/) and Socrative (http://www.socrative.com/) provide ways to ask multiple choice questions, as well as fill-in-the-blank and essay questions. Each also examines the answers to content-based multiple-choice questions, and reports the percentage of students who answered a question correctly.

Post-assessment data can easily be compared to pre-assessment data when the same questions are used in both. This data can be

> 1. I learned that Bessie Smith had an amazing life when growing up and had a beautiful voice one like no others.
>
> 2. I learned that during the Harlem Renaissance they had many improvements with money. Many got homes and jobs but there was still a lot of depression from not having the rights they got promised.
>
> — Seventh grade student

used to document student growth. Google Forms, and questions created in Socrative, can be downloaded and printed if computers are not available for student use. However, when students answer the questions by hand rather than on the computer, the reports feature will not work, unless the responses are then keyed into the online forms by a teacher or librarian.

Socrative also has a great app for schools that have tablet or laptop initiatives or participate in a Bring Your Own Device (BYOD) program. An additional online platform that has a great app for creating assessments is QuickTapSurvey (http://www.quicktapsurvey.com/).

> 1. I learned how to [use] Control F.
>
> 2. I learned that if you divide up the work and then share it, it goes a lot faster.
>
> — Seventh grade student

For those libraries with a BYOD policy at their school, there are a few online surveys that work well with all devices. These online surveys are free for educators at a basic level, and some offer upgraded services for a fee. Librarians would need to see if the basic requirements work for their respective schools.

- Kahoot! - (https://getkahoot.com/)

- Mentimeter - (https://www.mentimeter.com/)

- Poll Everywhere - (http://www.polleverywhere.com/)

There are many online platforms where surveys, online forms, and online quizzes can be created. The following is a list of some of the platforms that allow for the use of multiple question types, from drop-down menus and multiple choice, to fill-in-the-blank and multiple line text answers.

These are free accounts. Some also offer paid or fee-based upgrades to premium services, however, the free accounts will allow the creation of an assessment and generate reports of the responses.

- Kwik Surveys - (http://www.kwiksurveys.com/)

- Poll Everywhere - (http://www.polleverywhere.com/)

- SurveyMonkey - (http://www.surveymonkey.com/)

- Survs - (http://www.survs.com/)

No matter which instrument is used for assessment, librarians and teachers need to work with students to make sure formative and metacognitive assessments are taking place. Methods of assessment and the assessment process need to be explicitly taught to students for true reflection to occur. This reflection brings more meaning to the assessment, and demonstrates its value.

What to Include in an Assessment

For multimedia learning stations, a good assessment should include questions on content, concepts, research process, work process, and lesson "likability." There should be only a few of each type of question, because of the time constraints placed on the class. The self-assessments should not be linked to grades, unless an agreed-upon rubric was in place before the lesson.

Content assessment questions work best in multiple choice or essay form. With multiple choice questions used to gather content information, data can be collected between the pre- and post-assessments. The same content questions should appear on both pre- and post-assessments.

Example Content Questions:

1. Where did Duke Ellington play every week in Harlem during the Harlem Renaissance?

2. What is the probability that a basketball player will make his next free-throw attempt if he has successfully made 17 of his last 20 attempts?

Concept assessment questions allow students to reflect on their personal strengths and weaknesses for the day, and to ask for help where they need it. Either the teacher or the librarian should follow up on the individual weaknesses, so that learning is assured.

Example Concept Assessment Questions:

1. After today's lesson, what are you struggling with?

2. After today's lesson what do you feel you know really well?

Research process questions can be asked of students on both the pre- and post-self-assessments. The pre-assessment is a good time to ask students what they believe good resources are. The post-assessment can ask the same question, but must be followed up with additional questions about which resources they would use again, and why they are good to use.

Example Research Process Questions:

1. What are some good resources to use for research? (Pre- and Post-Assessments)

2. What are some good resources you used to research today that you can use again in the future? (Post-Assessment)

3. What makes using these resources better for research than using a general Google search? (Post-Assessment)

Learning process questions encourage student reflection. They ask students to look at the process they used to complete the multimedia learning stations, and to analyze it. They decide what they did well, and what they could do to improve their process in the future. It is also a good time to gauge whether or not students are becoming more resilient when they encounter difficulty. As the year goes on and students have more opportunities to experience multimedia learning stations, their resiliency should get stronger.

Example Learning Process Questions:

1. If you were to do this lesson again, what would you do differently?

2. When you were confused or had difficulty today, was it easy to go back and try again?

Finally, questions about what students thought of the lesson should be included. Librarians and teachers need feedback from students to see if the methods they are using are effective and engaging. Other than using observational skills, asking for this feedback is a good way to determine whether students were engaged, to find out which learning stations they liked and which ones they didn't like, and to gather student suggestions as to what was effective and what wasn't. This information is important for the librarian's own self reflection and future lesson revision.

Example Lesson "Likability" Questions:

1. Which of today's learning stations were the most engaging?

2. At which learning stations did you feel you learned the most?

3. What (kindly worded) suggestions do you have for improving this lesson for the future?

Additional Assessment in the Classroom

Ultimately, the classroom teacher decides how to assess students' learning for the day. When teachers go back to the classroom, they need to hold students accountable for their learning and

> As a teacher, I love the accountability that the lessons provide for my teams' growth measures. Everyone knows that teachers loathe the word "data," and are looking for ways to measure it that aren't left up to a 40-question multiple-choice test. Not all of our students excel in testing, so we need other ways to measure growth. When we set up for a library lesson, we already know that there will be pre- and post-data available for us. Students will walk into a lesson knowing very little about a subject, but become so engaged in the lesson that they leave having learned so much.
>
> Jen has the kids start off a station lesson in a very easy, calm way. There is a system that she sets up for them follow, one that every teacher who struggles with classroom management should seek to mimic. While students may come in exasperated from their journey to a room other than what they are used to, they are quickly immersed into that library vibe and are right at work. Computers are on, seats are taken, and the pre-assessment is up. This is not a difficult assessment. Rather, it's right to the point: What do you know about this topic before rotating through stations? I prefer to have my students go through library stations at the beginning of a unit, because this also serves to provide great data for county-mandated unit plans, and personal growth measures.
>
> Students often complain that they don't know any of the information that's on the pre-assessment, which offers a great opportunity for me (the teacher) to rotate around and ask questions. "Well, if you don't know about that now, what do you think we'll talk about today?" or reassure them that "it's OK if you don't know this now. Just try your best! Maybe by the end of the day you'll know all about this person/ place/event." A little over an hour later, they take the same assessment (now post), and all their progress is recorded.
>
> This became such a useful tool, that I started using Google Forms (the method Jen uses for pre- and post-assessments) to show the same kind of growth before and after my units, or even just mini-lessons. Class data is broken down into easy-to-read graphs by Google automatically, and individual progress can be read in an Excel chart made up from answers.
>
> Not only have I enjoyed using this tool to help me assess where remediation is needed, but it's been a great tool to show pre-/post-data to my administration.
>
> — Megan Peoples, history teacher

the processes they used during the day. Teachers use a variety of ways to hold students accountable. Some teachers grade every single question for accuracy. Others provide a short open-book quiz of 10 questions from all sections of the learning stations that is graded for accuracy. Some teachers give an effort grade, and some use a rubric. There are many ways teachers can summatively assess multimedia learning stations. For the librarian though, the formative and metacognitive data from the pre- and post-self-assessment is the most important and most informative.

Steps to Create Multimedia Learning Stations

Steps for Creating Multimedia Learning Stations

Determine Purpose

The overall purpose of the chosen set of multimedia learning stations should first be determined in collaboration with the teacher. Is the purpose mainly for students to gather information pertaining to the standards? Is it research and information fluency? Is it critical thinking and problem solving to build on the standards learned in class? Or is it pure extension and enrichment?

Also, the librarian and teacher will determine when the multimedia learning stations will be implemented within the scope and sequence of the unit. The learning stations' overall purpose and placement within the unit will dictate the types of sources used, and the types of questions asked of students.

Establish Topics

After the purpose has been decided, the teacher and librarian focus on selecting topics. The state curriculum standards and the Common Core standards (if applicable in the respective state) should be the guiding force in choosing these topics. If there is room, an extra learning station of interesting or "fun" facts, or a learning station of a more kinesthetic or playful nature can be included. Sometimes, immersing oneself in research before choosing topics will result in a number of exciting topics and themes. Other times it is better to choose topics first, then conduct the research.

Establish Creator

In preparing for multimedia learning stations, the librarian and teacher need to decide whether: (a) the librarian will plan and create the learning stations in their entirety, (b) the librarian and teacher will co-create the learning stations, or (c) the librarian and teacher will split up the learning stations, each creating different learning stations that will fit together to make the whole.

The librarian is the research expert, while the teacher is the content expert. Best practice is to employ a collaborative model for the planning and creation of stations, incorporating the strengths of the librarian and the teacher. Though in reality, time doesn't always allow for this type of collaboration, the goal should always be to get there.

Locate Sources

When locating and accessing sources for multimedia learning stations, it helps to search for the most difficult-to-find sources first. Educational apps and podcasts or audio broadcasts can be difficult to find for particular topics within a set of learning stations. Searching for the learning station topics in these sources first will result in more options to choose from.

Videos are the next most difficult types of sources to find. After matching these sources to topics within the learning stations, it is easier to find the remaining topics in databases, books, encyclopedias, and websites. Website sources can be saved for the most difficult topic to research, because of the plethora of information available online.

Create Directions and Questions

Once sources have been selected for each learning station topic, directions and questions can be created. The directions should be straightforward and simple to follow. The questions should address the "essential questions" for the topic being covered. They should be embedded with keywords taken directly from the content standards, or they should require students to answer with phrases that contain those keywords. A Bloom's Taxonomy Question Wheel can be used to help create questions. Whenever possible, thinking or discussion questions should be added, to encourage students to think beyond the facts. (See Chapter 5 for more information on Quality Questioning.)

Revise Work

Once the initial directions and questions have been created, revision work with the collaborating teacher can begin. Divide up the stations and have the teacher, co-librarian, a volunteer, or a student (who is not in the respective class) complete each station. Someone should complete each learning station to check for timing, phrasing, and proper usage and mechanics. Often a first draft learning station can be too long or too short for its intended purpose, and needs to be revised. This trial process will create streamlined stations that are free of any confusing phrasing or broken links.

Determine Rotation

After the learning stations have been edited and revised, the method of how students will rotate through the multimedia learning stations can be determined. Consider the grade level of the class, their experience with learning stations, and the timing of each one, to determine if some will take longer than others to successfully complete. Discuss with the teacher, to decide whether students will move through the stations at their own

> When students complete the stations at their own pace, we often create a rubric together that allows students to make choices as to which stations they will complete and submit for grading. This element allows room for differentiation and self-motivation, as well as the opportunity to spend more time with stations that speak to individual students' interests.
>
> — Shannon Hyman

pace, or if they will follow a timed rotation. Keep in mind that if using a timed rotation, students may or may not complete each station. Discuss with the teacher whether there will be more time given in class to complete any unfinished stations, or if the students' work will be assessed based on effort, completion, or accuracy.

Select Music

Incorporating music into learning stations is a great way to submerge students in an overall feeling of a time period or to give them another way to connect to their topic. If students are rotating from one learning station to the next in a timed fashion, using music as a rotation cue is very beneficial.

Songs from the Vietnam War era are good for Vietnam War Learning Stations. Elvis and the Beatles work well for *The Outsiders*, since the book is set in that time period, and both are mentioned in the novel. The rap song "Fractions" by Mr. Duey is good for Fractions learning stations. (It is also completely entertaining!) If students are rotating at their own place, it can be good for students to have this music playing at a particular learning station.

Students respond well to music. If a music clip isn't selected that pertains to the overall topic, one suggestion is to find a tone that fits the topic, or a song for students to rotate to, just for fun. During Anne Frank learning stations, slow, somber instrumental music or "Flight of the Valkyries" by Wagner—Hitler's composer of choice—can be played as a rotation cue. For Rocks and Minerals learning stations, rock and roll can be played.

Occasionally, if something cannot be found to match the topic in any way, clips from current music can be played for rotation, just for enjoyment and rotation cue purposes. A favorite is "I Like to Move It" by Reel 2 Real from the movie *Madagascar*.

Merge, Assemble, and Prepare Document

Once the directions and questions have been developed, they can be assembled into a packet. If a school has the capability, the packet can be in digital form and placed in a virtual learning repository for students to access, or it can be printed as a hard copy to distribute to each student.

Create Pre- and Post-Assessments

To show a pattern of growth in students, conducting pre- and post-assessments is essential. Within the pre- and post-assessments, content, as well as research and information fluency skills, can be addressed. Areas should be included for students to select which learning stations they found helpful, informative, and interesting, with another area provided for students to add comments or suggestions. This data informs the revision process for the following year, and for the creation of future learning stations.

Gather and Organize Materials

Computers, hand-held devices, DVD players, books, encyclopedias, or other materials needed to complete the learning stations should be pulled together and organized in a space where everything is kept together. In a school where there is a 1:1 technology initiative or a BYOD plan in place, there is more flexibility regarding how learning stations are set up, as well as whether the learning stations can be completed digitally via links. The materials gathered can be checked out by the teacher and completed in the classroom, if more time is needed. More information on organizing and implementing learning stations will be provided in Chapter 9.

Prepare Students

The classroom teacher should have students go directly to the library the day the multimedia learning stations will be conducted, in order to maximize the amount of time students will have to complete the lesson. Also, remind the teacher to ask students to bring their own earbuds or headphones the day the stations will be conducted.

Decide on Groups

How students are grouped for multimedia learning stations can be determined in various ways. Collaborating with the classroom teacher to determine how to split up the groups for the set of multimedia learning stations will give the best result.

Some common options for grouping students are to have the teacher choose groups to maximize the outcome for each student, to have students count off or draw a station out of a hat for a random sampling, or to have students select their own groups. There are benefits to each method, but to truly get to best experience, this decision should be made by the librarian and teacher, based on the personality of the class as a whole.

Steps for the Day of Multimedia Learning Stations

Pre-Assessment

Once students are situated with their required materials, they should take a brief pre-assessment covering the content they will be researching for the day, and the process they are familiar with when conducting research. Students need to be reminded that this pre-assessment activity is not graded. In fact, it's perfectly fine for them to write "IDK" or "I don't know" for their answers. They should be told that the purpose of the pre-assessment is to see how much they learn and grow from the beginning of class to the end, and that it is not an expectation that they already know material they haven't been taught yet. Another option, to save time, is that the pre-assessment can be performed in the classroom the day before the multimedia learning stations occur.

Learning Station Overview

After the brief pre-assessment, it will be time to go over each multimedia learning station. Beginning with Station 1, the librarian must go through all the learning stations, clearly stating the topic for each one, the resources required, and the focus for their research. It is necessary to give this overview and to tie it in to the overall unit and the standards that are being addressed within the classroom.

Learning Stations in Action

Students spend the class period researching the topics, answering and discussing questions, exploring the resources provided, and rotating through the various learning stations. The amount of time they have at each learning station depends on how long the pre-assessment and the overview take, plus how much time will be required for the post-assessment at the end.

Typically, getting situated, taking the pre-assessment, and going through the overview takes 15 minutes. The post-assessment at the end usually takes seven to eight minutes. Subtracting that time from the amount of time scheduled in a class period determines how long students will spend in each station. If enough time isn't available, the learning stations can be finished in the classroom the next day.

Post-Assessment

With seven or eight minutes left in the class period, students should complete a post-lesson self-assessment. The self-assessment should include content questions, process questions, and learning station preference questions. This data can then be compiled to assess the effectiveness of the learning stations in addressing purpose and process, and to inform revision of the multimedia learning stations for future classes. It can also serve the purpose of determining who may need extra help with the content or research, so that the librarian and/or teacher can be available for assistance and review.

1. Determine Purpose   Notes & Things to Do:

   • Gather Information

   • Research and Information Fluency

   • Critical Thinking and Problem Solving

   • Extension and Enrichment

   • Other _____

   &

   • Introduction

   • Middle of Unit

   • Review for Test

   • Culminating Activity

   • Enrichment

   • Other _____

2. Establish Topics

   • Brainstormed Topics

   • Researched Topics

   • Final Selection of Topics: Station 1, 2, 3, 4, 5, 6

3. Establish Creator(s)

   • Librarian

   • Librarian and Teacher Together

   • Divide and Conquer with Teacher

4. Locate Sources

   • Podcast/ Audio

   • Educational Apps

   • Videos

   • Databases

- Websites
- eBooks
- Images
- Music
- Print Sources
- Kinesthetic Activity
- Online Game
- Any Web 2.0 included?
- Other _____

5. Create Directions

- Station 1
- Station 2
- Station 3
- Station 4
- Station 5
- Station 6
- Other _____

6. Create Questions (Circle or Highlight Question Type)

- Station 1: Informational, Thinking, Discussion, Other
- Station 2: Informational, Thinking, Discussion, Other
- Station 3: Informational, Thinking, Discussion, Other
- Station 4: Informational, Thinking, Discussion, Other
- Station 5: Informational, Thinking, Discussion, Other
- Station 6: Informational, Thinking, Discussion, Other
- Other _____

7. Revise Work (Circle or Highlight the Reviser)

- Station 1: Student, Teacher, Volunteer, Other
- Station 2: Student, Teacher, Volunteer, Other
- Station 3: Student, Teacher, Volunteer, Other
- Station 4: Student, Teacher, Volunteer, Other
- Station 5: Student, Teacher, Volunteer, Other
- Station 6: Student, Teacher, Volunteer, Other
- Other _____

(Continued)

8. Determine Rotation   Notes & Things to Do:

- Timed Rotation: Music or No Music

- Untimed Rotation – All MMLS

- Untimed Rotation – Students Choose MMLS

9. Select Music

- Within MMLS

- As Rotation

- Does it pertain to the topic? Yes or No

10. Merge, Assemble, and Prepare Document

- Digital

- Print

11. Create Pre- and Post-Assessments

- Pre-Student Self-Assessment

- Post-Student Self-Assessment

12. Gather and Organize Materials

- Bin Labeled

- File folder Created

   ◦ Materials Needed List

   ◦ Library Layout

   ◦ Packet of MMLS

- Print Materials Gathered

13. Prepare Students

- Reminded to bring headphones

- Reminded to meet in library for class

14. Determine How Groups Will Work

- Teacher Selected

- Count Off

- Student Choice

Multimedia Learning Stations Preparation Checklist

1. Individual Learning Stations Set Up
   - Signs for MMLS
   - Headphones signs
   - Materials on Each Learning Station
     ◦ Station 1
     ◦ Station 2
     ◦ Station 3
     ◦ Station 4
     ◦ Station 5
     ◦ Station 6
     ◦ Other _____
2. Signage
   - Welcome sign
   - Sign to direct students where to put their stuff
   - Sign for things students need
   - Introductory directions for pre- student self-assessment (SSA)
   - Closure directions for post SSA
3. Equipment
   - Headphones bin ready with wipes for cleaning
   - Devices charges
   - Videos loaded
   - Music ready
   - Online Stopwatch
4. Packets of Directions and Questions
   - Digital
   - Print
5. Groups
   - Teacher Assigned
   - Count Off
   - Student Choice

Checklist for MMLS Day

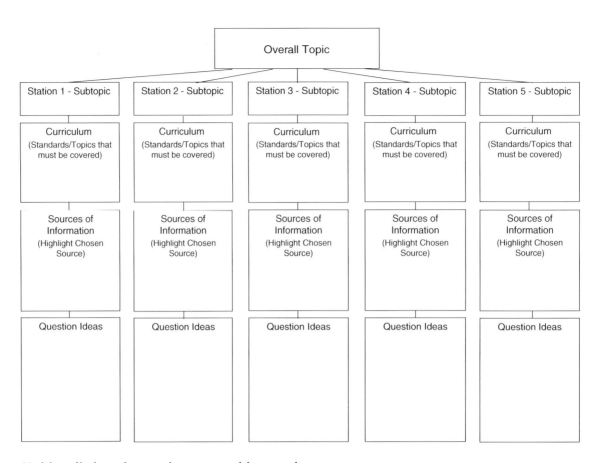

Multimedia learning stations — graphic organizer

9

Organization and Implementation

Keeping multimedia learning stations organized is extremely important. The vast amount of materials required, the organization of the library, the preservation of the materials, and the decisions made each year, should all be organized and streamlined in order to ensure sustainability and replication of the learning stations from year to year. It is beneficial to have a combination of both print and digital organization.

Physical and Print Organization

Bins are effective for holding print and other physical materials, and can be easily labeled. Good bins can be found at Demco Library Supplies ("Colored File Pockets") or even at the Dollar Store. On each bin, a spot can be found to attach a temporary label for the learning stations that are in use. These labels are temporary, because it is impractical to have a permanent bin for each set of learning stations that are created throughout a school year.

File folders are a great way to organize paper files. Within each file folder, a paper version of the multimedia learning stations' questions and directions can be kept. On the left side, a stapled version of the list of materials needed can be placed at the top, and a library layout map can be stapled at the bottom. Similar to a seating chart, the library layout map is a simple aerial view of the library space. Marking with a pencil where each learning station goes allows for a last minute change or revision in the coming years.

This file folder guide will be invaluable when there is a need for keeping track of multiple sets of learning stations scheduled within a single day, and also for reusing learning stations in future. Taking the time to create these simple maps allows others to assist the librarian in setting up the learning stations in between classes, and makes replication in subsequent years a breeze. Once a successful setup has been determined, photographs can also be taken and placed in the folder to further exemplify the placement and flow for future lessons.

File Folder Layout

The library layout map can be stapled onto the file folder as a pocket. A laminated sign for labeling the learning stations can then be placed in the pocket. This label will be affixed to a bin to identify the set of learning stations contained within it. The folder can be filed in a filing cabinet once the learning stations have been completed for the year.

The next time the set of learning stations is used, the folder can be taken out and placed in a bin. The label can be affixed to the bin and the materials that are listed can be pulled from the library shelves or other places and also placed in the bin.

Bins

Materials are kept in their respective bins for the duration of the learning experience. Having numerous classes in the library throughout the days and weeks, creates a situation where there may be multiple sets of learning stations in progress throughout the course of a day or week. Choosing bins in different colors can make it easier to identify which bins to grab for a set of learning stations. For example, multimedia learning stations on the Vietnam War may be scheduled during first and third periods, *The Outsiders* learning stations may be conducted during second period, and Slope learning stations during fourth period. Keeping each topic in a specific color bin aids in identifying which bin to grab for which period.

Stands and Station Numbers

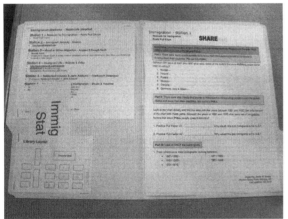

Each learning station should be clearly labeled. Placing signs in the middle of tables is an easy method of labeling. A sign can simply say "Station 1" to mark where students go. If the sign is elevated, students have an easier time determining where to rotate throughout the period. Scholastic Book Fairs offers elevated stands that work well for these signs. Also, students can quickly determine which learning stations require headphones, when headphones signs are placed at the appropriate location.

Headphones

File folder layout and organization

It is essential to recommend that students bring their own headphones or earbuds, but it is also imperative to have a class set available for students who don't bring them. (Individually wrapped alcohol swabs can be included at the learning station for cleaning in between use.)

Having a large container of headphones available for students at audio-centered learning stations is highly recommended. If headphones are not available, the sounds of the videos, podcasts,

A temporary label affixed to a bin that contains the books for a learning station

Signage for a multimedia learning station

Bin of headphones provided by the library

and/or audio files will quickly fill the library and distract other students. If a library only has one computer, TV, or tablet to show a video on, the device should either be placed away from other learning stations, or two to five students' headphones should be plugged into a headphone splitter, which plugs into the device. Belkin makes a great splitter called the Belkin Rockstar, which allows five pairs of headphones to be plugged into the same device.

Devices

Handheld devices and tablets should be kept where the teacher and/or librarian can easily monitor them. These devices includes eReaders, iPads, iPods, tablets, and other handheld devices of all kinds. Keeping track of them during rotations and before classes leave the library is necessary to ensure accountability of expensive equipment, and to make sure they remain charged and ready for the next group.

Digital Organization

For digital organization, an electronic copy of the learning stations, materials needed, and directions for students can be kept together in a file folder on a computer. As the learning stations are updated and/or changed, the previous versions can be deleted or stored in a file labeled "Old Stations." It can be beneficial to keep old learning stations, if sections of the original are removed. Sometimes, the removed sections may be added back into the learning stations as they are revised from year to year.

URL Shorteners

TinyURL.com is a good option to shorten web addresses because you can rename the shorter website yourself instead of having a randomly chosen series of numbers and letters.

Many times during website learning stations, the URL (web address) is too long. Long URLs result in frustrating errors and misdirection when they must be retyped by students. Underscores (_) can also cause confusion in URLs because they don't show up clearly in a document once the URL has been turned into a link. URL shorteners can help combat this issue.

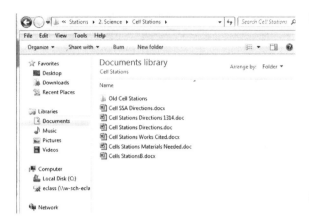

Digital file storage

An online egg timer to show students how much time is remaining in each timed learning station

Some good websites for turning long URLs into shorter ones are TinyURL (http://www.tinyurl.com), Google (https://goo.gl/), Bitly (https://bitly.com/), and Ow.ly (http://ow.ly/url/shorten-url). To ensure consistency for students, the librarian should use the same URL shortener for all lessons.

When creating a list of materials for a set of multimedia learning stations that include shortened URLs, both the original and the shortened URLs should be listed. Sometimes the URL of a website that is provided in set of multimedia learning stations changes over time, so the shortened URL won't work in future years. When the website changes, the original source can often be found by going to the homepage of the original website.

Online Timer

Once materials for a set of multimedia learning stations are dispersed, an electronic timer can help students keep track of time. If an LCD projector is available, the timer can be displayed on a screen at the front of the library, so students can keep track of their time and practice their time management skills. Different versions of an online timer can be Googled. Searching for "online egg timer" or "timer 5 minutes" will retrieve many suitable results.

Ideal Numbers and Group Organization

Multimedia learning stations tend to be most effective with three to six students in a group, depending on the amount of materials that are available, and how well students work in teams. The number of learning stations that are best for a topic vary, depending on the age of students, experience of students with the learning station process, experience of the students with the resources within the stations, the breadth of the topic, and the number of resources.

For younger students, fewer learning stations are recommended. Sixth grade students work best with three or four learning stations, while twelfth grade students can navigate through twice as many in the same amount of time. The more inexperienced the users are, the fewer learning stations can be completed within an allotted amount of time.

Multimedia learning stations conducted at the beginning of the year should be fewer in number than those conducted at the end of the year, because of the level of experience students may have had with the learning station process and the resources they will be searching within them.

Organize Students

Streamlining the items students carry from one learning station to the next facilitates easier transitions. When students enter the library, a sign can direct them where to go and where to drop off their things. A second sign can tell them what materials are required for the day. They may take those materials to the library tables and begin to follow the directions provided for the multimedia learning stations that they will be completing for the day.

Return Materials

Once a set of multimedia learning stations has been successfully completed in the library, the materials need to be put away for subsequent years. Any copies of print books can be noted on the "materials needed" list by title, author, and call number.

Introductory signage inside the front library doors to tell students where to put their things upon entering

Signage showing students what materials they need to take to the learning station areas

It also helps to put a small sticker on the spine of the book to indicate the book is used in a set of learning stations. A small red dot stands out, but isn't overbearing. This sticker placement can help when searching for the book in following years, but also in the weeding process. If the book is being weeded, another source will need to be purchased. It is better to know it needs replacing when it is weeded, rather than discovering that it is missing when the book is needed immediately for a set of learning stations.

Red dots on the top of the spine of each book used in a set of multimedia learning stations

The file folder containing all the information for the learning stations should already be prepped and ready to put away. Notes for future years, based on the operation of this year's learning stations, should be placed in the folder. The data for these notes can come from observation, practice, and/or the student post-self-assessment.

It is also beneficial to schedule a time to meet with the collaborating teacher, to determine any modifications this lesson may require for the future.

Part II

Example Sets of Multimedia Learning Stations

English 1

Anne Frank Learning Stations

Grade Level: 8–10

Subject Standards from Virginia Standards of Learning

English: http://www.doe.virginia.gov/testing/sol/standards_docs/english/index.shtml

8th Grade – 8.6, 8.9
9th Grade – 9.5, 9.8
10th Grade – 10.5, 10.8

AASL Standards

1 - Inquire, think critically, and gain knowledge

- 1.1 Skills - 1.1.1, 1.1.2, 1.1.6, 1.1.7, 1.1.8, 1.1.9

- 1.2 Dispositions in Action - 1.2.1, 1.2.6, 1.2.7

- 1.3 Responsibilities - 1.3.4, 1.3.5

2 - Draw conclusions, make informed decisions, apply knowledge to new situations, and create new knowledge

- 2.1 Skills - 2.1.3, 2.1.5

- 2.2 Dispositions in Action - 2.2.4

- 2.3 Responsibilities - 2.3.1, 2.3.3

- 2.4 Self-Assessment Strategies - 2.4.1, 2.4.2, 2.4.3, 2.4.4

3 - Share knowledge and participate ethically and productively as members of our democratic society

- 3.1 Skills - 3.1.1, 3.1.2, 3.1.3, 3.1.6

- 3.2 Dispositions in Action - 3.2.1, 3.2.2, 3.2.3

- 3.4 Self-Assessment Strategies - 3.4.1, 3.4.3

Modifications for Special Education Students:

1. Station 1 - Move this to the end of the lesson. Have students come back together. Listen to this podcast as a class and discuss.

2. Station 3 - Before the rotations begin for learning stations, watch the Otto Frank video interview as a class and discuss. His accent sometimes makes it difficult to interpret what is being said. Students benefit from a class discussion of what he and the interviewer talk about.

3. Station 4 - Remove Parts II and III.

4. Station 6 - Work with students at this station to work through similarities and differences.

Station 1 – Liberation

Method of Research: Listening to a podcast/radio broadcast for information

Highest Bloom's Taxonomy Level: Evaluating

Information to Research:

1. The British soldiers were filled with what emotion?

2. When one of the children in camp rolled up his sleeve, what was on his arm?

3. What were some of the occupations (jobs) of the people housed in the concentration camps before they became prisoners?

4. What song did the victims of the concentration camps play in their rescuers' honor?

5. The food rations for one American meal is as much food as the people in the camps would normally get for _____ days.

6. What did Winston Churchill say to the reporter about President Roosevelt?

7. **THINKING QUESTIONS:**

   - What is the most important thought you had after listening to this broadcast?

   - Can anyone like you or I really "understand" what life in the camps was like? Why or why not?

   - How can we, as humans, learn to understand others more completely?

Station 2 – The Secret Annex

Method of Research: Searching websites, video, and pictures for information

Highest Bloom's Taxonomy Level: Evaluating

Information to Research:

1. What is the number one tourist destination in Amsterdam today?

2. When was the Frank family betrayed?

3. What did Anne Frank die of? How old was she?

4. Into how many languages has Anne Frank's diary been translated?

5. Where would the occupants of the secret annex go on the weekends?

6. What did they do there?

7. Why did Otto Frank want the secret annex to stay empty? What does it symbolize?

8. **THINKING QUESTION:** Do you agree with keeping the secret annex empty? Why or why not?

Part II Directions:
- Independently go to http://tinyurl.com/secretannex
- Click through the links on the left side to see images of the rooms in the Secret Annex.
- Describe your thoughts and reactions in a paragraph of at least five complete sentences.

Your thoughts and reactions:

Station 3 – Miep Gies and Otto Frank

Method of Research: Reading a text interview and watching a video interview to find information

Highest Bloom's Taxonomy Level: Evaluating

Directions: You may do this station independently, work with a partner, or work with your whole group.

Miep Gies Directions: Go to http://tinyurl.com/miepinterview to read an interview with Miep Gies, and answer the questions below.

Information to Research:

1. How did Miep feel about having to hide the Franks? [**Note:** In this long section, you will need to scan the questions asked in the interview first, to get a sense of which ones will help you answer this question best.]

2. Scroll down to "The Capture." Read this part of the interview. What happened the day the Franks and others were captured?

3. Who turned in the Franks and the others living in the Secret Annex?

4. What happened to the Franks' possessions?

5. **THINKING QUESTION:** What did you learn from this interview that most intrigued you?

6. **THINKING QUESTION:** Suppose you were in Miep's position during the World War II. Would you have hidden the Franks, knowing how much was at risk? Explain.

Otto Frank Directions: Go to http://tinyurl.com/ottofrankinterview to watch a televised interview with Otto Frank conducted by the BBC, and answer the questions below.

Information to Research:

1. How many volumes of Anne's diary were there?

2. Has he ever regretted publishing Anne's diary?

3. How did Mr. Frank really learn to know Anne?

4. What is the purpose of the Anne Frank foundation?

5. How often did Anne's diary give Mr. Frank inspiration and courage?

6. **RESPONSE:** What was your experience, seeing the real Otto Frank being interviewed?

7. **THINKING QUESTION:** What choice would you have made about publishing Anne's diary, if you were her father? Explain why that would be your choice.

Station 4 – Hitler and Holocaust Statistics

Method of Research: Watching a video and reading an eBook and a website for information

Highest Bloom's Taxonomy Level: Analyzing

> **Part I Directions:** Go to http://tinyurl.com/speechhitleryouth to watch a video from the United States Holocaust Memorial Museum, of Hitler giving a speech at a youth rally in Thuringia on June 18, 1933.

Information to Research:

1. Describe Hitler's body language during this speech.

2. Describe your reaction and thoughts on this video. Write at least two complete sentences.

3. **THINKING QUESTION:** Why can't you understand what Hitler is saying?

Next: Read the Description to the right of the video

1. How many people were in the crowd to see Hitler?

2. This is an outdoor youth rally. In your own words, what does youth mean?

3. **THINKING QUESTION:** Why do you think Hitler found it so important or valuable to have youths support him?

> **Part II Directions:** Working with your group, use the eBooks provided about Hitler, Kristallnacht, and/or the "Final Solution" to answer the questions.

Information to Research:

1. Give at least two reasons why the German people supported Hitler.

2. Name three things that were destroyed or damaged during Kristallnacht.

3. What kind of Europe had Hitler envisioned, and who was to be removed in this Europe?

4. As part of the "Final Solution," Jewish people were told they were going to be resettled. Where were they sent?

5. **THINKING QUESTION:** Based on the information you found, what do you think Hitler wanted for Germany?

> **Part III Directions:** Working with your group, go to http://tinyurl.com/holostats and use the statistics to answer the questions.

Information to Research:

1. What was the total number of Jews in in these countries prior to the Holocaust?

2. How many were left after the Holocaust?

3. Which country had the highest percentage in loss of lives?

4. **THINKING QUESTION:** What questions do you have after looking at these statistics?

Station 5 – Concentration Camps

Method of Research: Searching pictures on a website and interpreting information

Highest Bloom's Taxonomy Level: Analyzing

> **Directions:**
> - Independently go to http://www.remember.org/camps/
> - Select "List of Photos" under Birkenau or Mauthausen
> - Spend ten minutes quietly searching through these pictures and reading the captions.
> - Do not discuss what you see with your group members. This is a time for quiet, personal reflection.
> - After ten minutes, record some things you saw in the pictures and your reactions to those images. This must be in at least five complete sentences. You may write about your feelings, something that surprised you, something that horrified you, etc.

Your reactions (remember to use at least five complete sentences):

Station 6 – Children of the Holocaust

Method of Research: Reading eBooks for information

Highest Bloom's Taxonomy Level: Analyzing

> **Directions:** Working with your group, use the eBooks on the Holocaust to answer the questions. You may use a computer or a tablet to access the eBooks.

Information to Research:

1. What was life like for children living in the ghettos?

2. What was life like for children in concentration camps?

3. What was life like for children in hiding?

4. Compare and contrast the life of a child in the ghetto, in a concentration camp, and in hiding. To do this, you will need to find information in the eBooks on what life was like for a child in each of these settings. Work with your group and fill in the Venn diagram together.

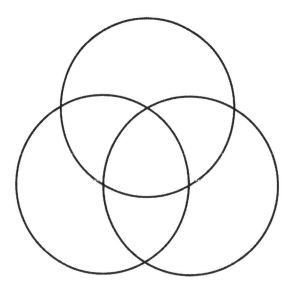

Venn Diagram

Materials Needed for Anne Frank Learning Stations

Station 1 – Liberation – Podcast of National Public Radio Broadcast

- Website for a podcast from NPR: http://tinyurl.com/campliberation (original: http://www.npr.org/player/v2/mediaPlayer.html?action=1&t=1&islist=false&id=4630493&m=4630494);

- Headphones

- Headphones sign

Station 2 – The Secret Annex – Website, Video and Pictures

- Video: "Visiting the Anne Frank House" (NBC TODAY show): http://tinyurl.com/afrankhousetoday (original: https://archives.nbclearn.com/portal/site/k-12/browse/?cuecard=53641)

- Website: http://tinyurl.com/secretannex (original: http://www.annefrankguide.net/en-GB/bronnenbank.asp?aid=10696)

- Headphones

- Headphones sign

Station 3 – Miep Gies and Otto Frank – Website and Video

- Website: http://tinyurl.com/miepinterview (original: http://teacher.scholastic.com/frank/tscripts/miep.htm);

- Video: Otto Frank Interview (originally from BBC): http://tinyurl.com/ottofrankinterview (original: http://www.bbc.co.uk/archive/holocaust/5095.shtml OR https://www.youtube.com/watch?v=T8PuzPAOVsA)

- Headphones

- Headphones sign

Station 4 – Hitler and Holocaust Statistics – Video, Website, and Book

- Hitler's Youth Rally Speech (USHMM – Steven Spielberg's Film Archives) http://tinyurl.com/speechhitleryouth (original: http://resources.ushmm.org/film/display/detail.php?file_num=746)

- eBooks on Hitler, Kristallnacht, and/or the "Final Solution"

- Website: http://tinyurl.com/holostats (original: http://www.historyplace.com/worldwar2/holocaust/h-statistics.htm)

- Headphones

- Headphones sign

Station 5 – Concentration Camps – Website

- Website: http://www.remember.org/camps

Station 6 – Children of the Holocaust – Books

- eBooks on the Holocaust and Children of the Holocaust

Rotation Song Suggestion: Something slow, soft, and mournful

Student Pre-Self-Assessment:

These questions are to be answered before the lesson takes place. The questions can be multiple choice for data collection purposes, or fill-in-the-blank.

1. What is a good source to use for historical research? (If you haven't learned this before or you don't know, put IDK.)

2. What happened during Kristallnacht? (If you haven't learned this before or you don't know, put IDK.)

3. What was The Final Solution? (If you haven't learned this before or you don't know, put IDK.)

4. Describe a concentration camp. (If you haven't learned this before or you don't know, put IDK.)

Post- Student Self-Assessment:

These questions are to be answered after the lesson takes place. Any or all of the following questions can be used in an assessment of your choice (see Chapter 6) for this set of multimedia learning stations. The questions can be multiple choice for data collection purposes or students may fill in the blank.

1. What is a good source to use for historical research?

2. What happened during Kristallnacht?

3. What was The Final Solution?

4. Describe something you learned today that you didn't already know about concentration camps.

5. What is something specific you learned today that surprised you?

6. Complete this sentence. "After today, I am still struggling with…"

7. What learning stations did you find to be the most interesting? Check all that apply.

- Station 1 - Liberation – Podcast of NPR Radio Broadcast

- Station 2 - The Secret Annex – Website, Video, & Pictures

- Station 3 - Miep Gies & Otto Frank – Website & Video

- Station 4 - Hitler & Holocaust Statistics – Video, Website, & Book

- Station 5 - Concentration Camps – Website

- Station 6 - Children of the Holocaust – Books

8. What would you change about your learning process if you were to do these stations again?

9. Overall, how would you assess your learning today?

- I did extremely well. I learned a lot about my topic and wonder about more. I learned some research skills to use in the future.

- I did well. I learned something about my topic and how to research in the future.

- I did OK. I could have worked a little harder, but I learned something about my topic and researching.

- I wasn't on my game today. I didn't learn nearly as much as I could have.

- I didn't do anything today, so I didn't learn anything.

10. Kindly list any suggestions you have for improving these stations.

Big Project Assessment Option:

Student Directions

Graphic novels and comic books are different from one another. Graphic novels are fiction or nonfiction books written and illustrated in a comic book format. They have a storyline and a plot that lasts the entire book. Comic books are serialized. Think of comics in a newspaper. The same comic doesn't usually continue the same plot week after week. The story in a comic book is short and generally changes every few strips.

Graphic novels can be about serious subjects, written in a serious tone. They don't have to be funny.

There are many graphic novels about the Holocaust. Look through some examples. You can look at the print books or eBooks in the school library or the public library for examples of format and tone.

Working in groups of four, you will be creating a section of a graphic novel about Anne Frank. You will be using an online comic generator. Each group member is in charge of one section for the whole group and will be graded on his or her section. Each group member will create a six- to eight-pane section of a graphic novel, covering one of four topics.

Topic 1 - Daily Life in the Secret Annex

Topic 2 - The Capture

Topic 3 - The Concentration Camp

Topic 4 - Otto's Return and Decision to Publish Anne's Diary

Notes for Librarian and/or Teacher:

1. Students should be provided with some examples of graphic novels covering World War II. Here are some examples, but there are many available online and in your respective libraries.

- *Maus I: A Survivor's Tale: My Father Bleeds History* by Art Spiegelman

- *Maus II: A Survivor's Tale: And Here My Troubles Began* by Art Spiegelman

- *Anne Frank: The Anne Frank House Authorized Graphic Biography* by Sidney Jacobson

- *Yossel: April 19, 1943* by Joe Kubert
- *I Was a Child of Holocaust Survivors* by Bernice Eisenstein
- *Mendel's Daughter: A Memoir* by Martin Lemelman

2. They should also be given a list of Web 2.0 tools for comic generators. Here is a list of examples. Some allow students to draw the strips from scratch, others turn photos into comic format, and others allow students to drag and drop characters, setting, etc.

- BeFunky - http://www.befunky.com/
- Chogger - http://chogger.com/
- Comic Master - http://plasq.com/apps/comiclife/macwin/
- Make Beliefs Comix - http://www.makebeliefscomix.com/
- Pixton - http://www.pixton.com/
- Toonlet - http://toonlet.com/
- Write Comics - http://writecomics.com/

3. A rubric should be created based on what outcomes are required for the particular grade level completing the project.

English 2

The Giver Learning Stations

Created in collaboration with Carolyn Stenzel

Grade Level: 7–10

Subject Standards from Virginia Standards of Learning

English: http://www.doe.virginia.gov/testing/sol/standards_docs/english/index.shtml

7th Grade – 7.6, 7.9
8th Grade – 8.6, 8.9
9th Grade – 9.5, 9.8
10th Grade – 10.5, 10.8

AASL Standards

Inquire, think critically, and gain knowledge

- 1.1 Skills – 1.1.6, 1.1.7, 1.1.8, 1.1.9

- 1.2 Dispositions in Action – 1.2.1, 1.2.6, 1.2.7

- 1.3 Responsibilities – 1.3.4, 1.3.5

Draw conclusions, make informed decisions, apply knowledge to new situations, and create new knowledge

- 2.1 Skills – 2.1.3, 2.1.5

- 2.2 Dispositions in Action – 2.2.3, 2.2.4

- 2.3 Responsibilities – 2.3.1, 2.3.2, 2.3.3

- 2.4 Self-Assessment Strategies – 2.4.1, 2.4.3

Share knowledge and participate ethically and productively as members of our democratic society

- 3.1 Skills – 3.1.3, 3.1.5, 3.1.6

- 3.2 Dispositions in Action – 3.2.1, 3.2.2, 3.2.3

- 3.3 Responsibilities – 3.3.1, 3.3.2, 3.3.3, 3.3.5

- 3.4 Self-Assessment Strategies – 3.4.1, 3.4.3

Note to Librarian: Before students conduct these learning stations, a discussion should take place on utopian versus dystopian societies. The possibilities, the realities, and the reasons for trying to create them should be discussed. They will be looking at different cultures and laws created with the purpose of improving situations. Some of them are less successful than others.

Modifications for Special Education Students:

1. Stations 1 and 5 – Talk to them about what benefits and drawbacks are. Make sure they understand that they are to read the article and figure out what is a benefit and what is a drawback. They are not searching for an answer; they are determining one.

2. Station 2 – students will need help indexing with print books and doing a keyword search with an eBook. Have a facilitator help lead this discussion, rather than requiring printed answers.

3. Station 4 – Remove in order to provide more time at the other learning stations.

4. Station 6 – Show students how to access the transcript of the podcast, so that they can read it while they listen, if they prefer.

5. Remove the citation requirements unless they have learned how to do this in previous research lessons.

Station 1 – Amish

Method of Research: Searching and reading subscription databases for information

Highest Bloom's Taxonomy Level: Analyzing

> **Directions:**
> *   Use the school subscription databases to search for articles on the Amish.
> *   Select an article on the Amish.
> *   Use the information from the article to answer the questions.
> *   If you can't find all of the answers, go back and try another article from your search results.

Information to Research:

1. What is the basic background/history of the Amish?

2. How is the Amish culture different from mainstream American culture?

3. Why do the Amish want to separate themselves from the rest of society?

4. Cite your source. Sometimes the citation is included in the database article. If it isn't, go to EasyBib (www.easybib.com) to create a citation.

5. **THINKING QUESTION:** What are some benefits to the Amish lifestyle? What are some drawbacks?

Benefits	Drawbacks

Station 2 – China's One-Child Policy

Method of Research: Searching and reading eBooks for information

Highest Bloom's Taxonomy Level: Evaluating

Information to Research:

1. What is China's one-child policy?

2. Why did the Chinese government create this law?

3. What exceptions are there to the one-child policy?

4. How does this policy impact people's lives? (How does it affect parents' lives? A child's? Community life?)

5. **THINKING QUESTIONS:**

    a. What kind of problems could be created by only allowing people to have one child?

    b. Do you think the one-child policy will help Chinese society? Explain.

    c. How would you feel if you knew you could only have one child? OR: If you have siblings, how would it feel to be without them?

Station 3 – Cloning

Method of Research: Watching and listening to a video for information

Highest Bloom's Taxonomy Level: Evaluating

Directions:

- Login to http://www.discoveryeducation.com.
- Type "Ethics of Human Cloning" in the search box and select Search.
- Select the video "The Ethics of Human Cloning" (5:39).
- Put on your headphones.
- Watch and listen to the video and answer the questions.
- You may PAUSE as you go to answer the questions.

Information to Research:

1. How has technology advanced to create the possibility of cloning?

2. How is a clone created?

3. Why do some people support cloning?

4. Why are some people against cloning?

5. **THINKING QUESTION:** What is your opinion on cloning? Support your answer with detailed reasons.

Station 4 – Climate Control

Method of Research: Using a definition and website to inspire thought and find information

Highest Bloom's Taxonomy Level: Analyzing

Directions:
- Use a dictionary (print or electronic) to look up the definition for "Climate control."
- Use the definition, then think about and answer the questions below.

Information to Research:

What does *climate control* mean?

THINKING QUESTION: Give some examples of what is already climate controlled in our world. (See definition above.)

THINKING QUESTION: What is not climate controlled in our world?

THINKING QUESTION: What are some pros and cons of humans living in a world that is completely climate controlled (even outside)?

Pros	Cons

Directions: Go to the website: http://tinyurl.com/biodomeca to learn more about biodomes and climate-controlled environments.

Information to Research:

What is a biodome?

Directions:
- Select "Nature Under Glass" at the bottom of the page.
- Select the different ecosystems to take a virtual tour. You will see a 360-degree camera rotation.

THINKING QUESTIONS:

1. What are some reasons for creating a biodome/greenhouse?
2. What would it be like if our whole world existed inside a massive biodome?

Station 5 – Communes and Communal Living

Method of Research: Searching and reading subscription databases for information

Highest Bloom's Taxonomy Level: Evaluating

> **Directions:**
> - Search the subscription databases for articles on communes or communal living
> - Select an article on communes or communal living.
> - Use the information from the article to answer the questions.
> - If you can't find all of the answers, go back and try another result.

Information to Research:

1. What is a commune?

2. How is living in a commune different from the way most people live?

3. What are the benefits of communal living?

4. What are the drawbacks of communal living?

5. Cite your source. You may find a citation already completed in the database article. If not, go to EasyBib (www.easybib.com) to create a citation.

6. **THINKING QUESTION:** What is your opinion of a commune or communal living? Would you choose to live that way? Why or why not?

Station 6 – North Korea

Method of Research: Listening to a podcast for information

Highest Bloom's Taxonomy Level: Evaluating

> **Directions:** Listen to the NPR podcast at the following website to learn more about North Korea: http://tinyurl.com/nkpodcast.

Information to Research:

1. How is North Korea different from much of the rest of the world?

2. What does the government control in North Korea?

3. Are people allowed to leave North Korea?

4. How do North Koreans get their information?

THINKING QUESTIONS:

1. Why do you think the North Korean government doesn't grant its people some of the freedoms we have in the United States?

2. Do you think the North Korean people are aware of a different life outside of North Korea?

3. Why do you think the author and the interviewer visualize North Korea in all gray?

Materials Needed for *The Giver* Learning Stations

Station 1 – Amish – Subscription Databases

- School subscription databases – general search on "Amish"

Station 2 – China's One-Child Policy – eBooks

- eBooks on China
- May also include print books and encyclopedias, if desired

Station 3 – Cloning – Discovery Education Video

- Discovery Education Video – "The Ethics of Human Cloning"
- Headphones

Station 4 – Climate Control – Dictionary and Website

- Online or print dictionary
- Space for Life Biodôme website: http://tinyurl.com/montbiodome (original: http://espacepourlavie.ca/en/biodome)

Station 5 – Communes and Communal Living – Subscription Databases

- School subscription databases – general search on "communal living"

Station 6 – North Korea – Podcast

- NPR Podcast – "Graphic Novel Depicts Surreal North Korea": http://tinyurl.com/nkpodcast (original: http://www.npr.org/templates/story/story.php?storyId=6256290)
- Headphones

Student Pre-Self-Assessment:

These questions are to be answered before the lesson takes place. The questions can be multiple choice for data collection purposes, or students may fill in the blank.

1. What is a good source to use for research? (If you haven't learned this yet or you don't know, put IDK.)
2. What is cloning? (If you haven't learned this yet or you don't know, put IDK.)
3. How do North Koreans live differently than Americans? (If you haven't learned this yet or you don't know, put IDK.)
4. What policy does China use to control its population growth? (If you haven't learned this yet or you don't know, put IDK.)

Student Post-Self-Assessment:

These questions are to be answered after the lesson takes place. Any or all of the following questions can be used in an assessment of your choice (see Chapter 6) for this set of multimedia learning stations. The questions can be multiple choice for data collection purposes, or students may fill in the blank.

1. What is a good source to use for research?

2. What is cloning?

3. How do North Koreans live differently than Americans?

4. What policy does China use to control population growth?

5. What is something specific you learned today that surprised you?

6. What learning stations did you find to be the most interesting? Check all that apply.

   • Station 1 - Amish - Subscription Databases

   • Station 2 - China's One-Child Policy - eBooks

   • Station 3 - Cloning - Discovery Education Video

   • Station 4 - Climate Control - Dictionary and Website

   • Station 5 - Communes and Communal Living - Subscription Databases

   • Station 6 - North Korea - Podcast

7. What would you change about your learning process if you were to do these stations again?

8. Overall, how would you assess your learning today?

   • I did extremely well. I learned a lot about my topic and would like to learn more. I learned some research skills to use in the future.

   • I did well. I learned something about my topic and gained some tips on how to research in the future.

   • I did OK. I could have worked a little harder, but I learned something about my topic and about researching.

   • I wasn't on my game today. I didn't learn nearly as much as I could have.

   • I didn't do anything today, so I didn't learn anything.

9. Kindly list any suggestions you have for improving these stations:

Big Project Assessment Option:

Using the research from these learning stations, have students choose elements of these societies they would use to create their own idea for a utopian society. Students can build a website promoting their society to encourage others to become a part of it. They should also include a piece explaining what problems the society may encounter on its route to attempted perfection.

To create a website, use Weebly (http://www.weebly.com/) or Google Sites (https://sites.google.com).

Two examples of websites created by communes attempting to have a more perfect society are below.

Twin Oaks Community - http://www.twinoakscommunity.org/

Fellowship of International Community - http://www.ic.org/

English 3

Milkweed Learning Stations

Grade Level: 7–9

Subject Standards from Virginia Standards of Learning

English: http://www.doe.virginia.gov/testing/sol/standards_docs/english/index.shtml

7th Grade – 7.6, 7.9
8th Grade – 8.6, 8.9
9th Grade - 9.5, 9.8

AASL Standards

1 - Inquire, think critically, and gain knowledge

- 1.1 Skills – 1.1.2, 1.1.6, 1.1.7, 1.1.8, 1.1.9
- 1.2 Dispositions in Action – 1.2.6
- 1.3 Responsibilities – 1.3.5
- 1.4 Self-Assessment Strategies – 1.4.4

2 - Draw conclusions, make informed decisions, apply knowledge to new situations, and create new knowledge

- 2.1 Skills – 2.1.1, 2.1.3, 2.1.5, 2.1.6
- 2.2 Dispositions in Action – 2.2.4
- 2.4 Self-Assessment Strategies – 2.4.2, 2.4.3, 2.4.4

3 - Share knowledge and participate ethically and productively as members of our democratic society

- 3.1 Skills – 3.1.3, 3.1.6
- 3.2 Dispositions in Action – 3.2.3
- 3.4 Self-Assessment Strategies – 3.4.1, 3.4.3

Modifications for Special Education Students:

1. Station 1 - Remove

2. Station 2 - Remove the eBook source, but keep the websites

3. Station 3 - Remove some of the questions (Hitler - take out questions 1, 4, 6, and 7; Himmler - take out questions 1, 5, and 6; Korczak - take out questions 1, 4, and 6)

4. Station 4 - Work with students through the questioning process to make the connections between the facts of the diseases they research and why they were rampant in the ghettos and concentration camps.

5. Station 5 - Ask for two testimonies rather than three.

6. Remove the citation requirements unless students have learned how to do this in previous research lessons.

Beginning Station – Warsaw, Poland 1939

Method of Research: Searching a video for information

Highest Bloom's Taxonomy Level: Understanding

Information to Research:

1. Where is Germany in relation to Poland?

2. When did Jewish people first arrive in Poland? Why did they arrive?

3. Whom did the Nazis target?

4. When the Nazis invaded Poland, where did they force Jewish people to live?

5. Where were they sent to die after the ghettos?

6. How long did the Jewish people in the Warsaw Ghetto fight off the Nazis during the Warsaw Ghetto Uprising?

7. How many Jewish rebels were killed? How many were taken to concentration camps?

8. Three million Jewish people lived in Poland before World War II. How many Jewish survivors were there after the war?

9. **CLASS DISCUSSION QUESTION:** What can you suppose and learn from the number of Jewish people living in Poland before the war compared to the number of Jewish survivors remaining in Poland after the war?

Station 1 – Geography of Warsaw and Berlin

Method of Research: Using an online atlas and Google Earth to understand distance

Highest Bloom's Taxonomy Level: Analyzing

Part 1 Directions: Look up Poland and Germany using an online atlas: http://www.worldatlas.com/aatlas/world.htm

Information to Research:

1. Where are the countries of Poland and Germany in relation to each other?

2. Use the "Driving Distances" section of the online atlas to find how many miles there are between Warsaw, Poland, and Berlin, Germany. http://www.worldatlas.com/travelaids/travelaids.htm How many miles are between Warsaw, Poland, and Berlin, Germany?

3. Use your math skills to calculate how long of a drive it would take to get from Warsaw to Berlin if the driver is driving at 60 miles per hour. How long of a drive would it be? _____

4. How is this distance connected to the large number of Polish Jews who were captured and set to ghettos and concentration camps?

Part 2 Directions:
- Open Google Earth and search for the city in which you live.
- Open the Ruler tool
- Select the city you live in with the ruler
- You can extend the ruler to determine distances. (Make sure you have set it to calculate miles.)
- Extend the ruler from the city you live in to another state. Make the distance equal to the same amount of miles as the distance between Warsaw and Berlin.

Information to Research:

1. What state did you reach? _____

2. **THINKING QUESTION:** Imagine driving to that state. That is the distance between these two cities. Would it be easy for the Germans to invade Warsaw with its large Jewish community? Explain your answer.

3. **THINKING QUESTION:** What would it be like to live that distance away from the headquarters of a country you are fighting against in a war?

Station 2 – Children of the Warsaw Ghetto

Method of Research: Searching photographs on websites and eBooks to visualize information

Highest Bloom's Taxonomy Level: Creating

> **Directions:** Go to Google Images and search for Children of the Warsaw Ghetto
> - OR You may look at pictures of the children of the Warsaw Ghetto in the eBooks provided.
> - Use these pictures to answer the questions and reflect on your thoughts.

1. Open and view at least 10 pictures of children from the Warsaw Ghetto. Describe what you see in the 10 pictures in a paragraph. (You are not writing 10 paragraphs. You are writing one paragraph to describe the overall feeling you get from the 10 images.) What do the children look like, where are they, what is happening, etc.? Your answer must be a paragraph of at least five complete sentences.

2. Pick one of the photos to react to in more detail. What is happening in the picture? How must the child(ren) be feeling? Write a paragraph in first person as if you are the child (or one of the children) in this photo. Your paragraph must be at least five complete sentences.

3. Describe which picture you chose.

Station 3 – Hitler, Himmler, Korczak

Method of Research: Searching databases for information

Highest Bloom's Taxonomy Level: Remembering

> **Directions:** Hitler, Himmler, and Korczak were characters in the novel Milkweed, but they were also real people. You will research them at this station. As a group divide up the three research subjects at this station. Each person should choose to research Hitler, Himmler or Korczak. You may discuss and share the information you find with each other. Make sure as a group you have researched all three people.

> **Student I Directions: Hitler:** Use the school subscription databases to search for articles on Hitler. You may use more than one article to find your information.

Information to Research:

1. When did Adolf Hitler become the Chancellor of Germany?

2. What are ways Hitler turned Germans against Jewish people?

3. What is genocide (you may look this up in a dictionary)?

4. What did Hitler and his advisors call their particular form of genocide?

5. What were concentration camps?

6. How many European Jews died by the end of World War II in 1945?

7. How and when did Adolf Hitler die?

8. **CITE YOUR SOURCE.** You should find a citation already created in the database, but if you don't, you may use EasyBib: http://www.easybib.com.

9. **THINKING QUESTION:** Would World War II have happened without Hitler?

> **Student II Directions: Himmler:** Use the school subscription databases to search for articles on Himmler. You may use more than one article to find your information.

Information to Research:

1. Heinrich Himmler took over the secret police, which were called _____.

2. After taking over the SA, what was one of Himmler's major duties?

3. Use a dictionary to define exterminate.

4. Whom did Himmler and his deputy order to be exterminated?

5. What order did Himmler issue in August 1941?

6. How and when did Heinrich Himmler die?

7. **CITE YOUR SOURCE.** You should find a citation already created in the database, but if you don't, you may use EasyBib: http://www.easybib.com.

8. **THINKING QUESTION:** Why did Himmler exterminate people?

> **Student III Directions: Dr. Korczak:** Use the school subscription databases to search for articles on Janusz Korczak. You may use more than one article to find your information.

Information to Research:

1. Korczak founded and ran an _____ for Jewish children in Poland.

2. Why did Korczak decline to go into hiding when his friends encouraged him to do so?

3. Did Korczak escape the Warsaw Ghetto when he had the chance? Why or why not?

4. Where were Korczak and his orphans sent when they were forced out of the ghetto?

5. How many of Korczak's orphans survived?

6. Where did Korczak die?

7. **CITE YOUR SOURCE.** You should find a citation already created in the database, but if you don't, you may use EasyBib: http://www.easybib.com.

8. **THINKING QUESTION:** Is Korczak a hero? Why or why not?

Station 4 – Diseases – Tuberculosis and Typhus

Method of Research: Searching subscription databases and a website for information

Highest Bloom's Taxonomy Level: Analyzing

> **Directions:** You will research as a group at this station. Half of your group should research tuberculosis and the other half should research typhus. You may discuss and share the information you find with each other, but the work must be split up evenly. If someone doesn't research and have information to contribute to the group, they may not use the answers of others in the group.

> **Part I Directions: Tuberculosis**
> - Use the school subscription databases to search for articles on tuberculosis. You may use more than one article to find your information.
> - Or you may use the following website to answer the questions below http://tinyurl.com/TBarticle.
> - You may need to use more than one of these sources to find the answers to the questions.

Information to Research:

1. What is tuberculosis?

2. When were drugs that could treat tuberculosis discovered?

3. **THINKING QUESTION:** Were these drugs available during World War II? Explain your answer.

4. **THINKING QUESTION:** Looking at the groups of people you have learned are more likely to get tuberculosis, why do you think this illness was so common in the ghettos during World War II?

5. How is tuberculosis spread from person to person?

6. What are some symptoms of tuberculosis?

7. **CITE YOUR SOURCES.** You should find a citation already created in the database, but if you don't or if you used the website, you may use EasyBib: http://www.easybib.com.

> **Part II Directions: Typhus**
> - Use the school subscription databases to search for articles on Typhus. You may use more than one article to find your information.
> - You may need to use more than one of these sources to find the answers to the questions.

Information to Research:

1. What is typhus?

2. What are some symptoms experienced by a person infected with typhus?

3. How is typhus contracted (meaning how does someone get typhus)?

4. **THINKING QUESTION:** Why do you think typhus was often contracted by people in the ghettos and concentration camps during World War II? Your answer must be in complete sentences.

5. **CITE YOUR SOURCE.** You should find a citation already created in the database, but if you don't, you may use EasyBib: http://www.easybib.com.

Station 5 – Testimonies of Survivors of the Warsaw Ghetto

Method of Research: Watching videos on a reliable website for understanding

Highest Bloom's Taxonomy Level: Understanding

> **Directions:**
> - You will work on this station independently.
> - Go to http://tinyurl.com/warsawtestimonies to go to a website to find testimonies of survivors of the Warsaw Ghetto.
> - Choose and watch at least three testimonies and record your thoughts.
> - If the video doesn't load, read the transcript to the right of the video to see what the person said.
> - (You don't have to watch the first three listed. It can *be any* three.)

Information to Research:

1. Testimony 1:

   - What was the name of this survivor?

   - What did he/she talk about?

   - What are your thoughts and feelings about this person's experience?

2. Testimony 2:

   - What was the name of this survivor?

   - What did he/she talk about?

   - What are your thoughts and feelings about this person's experience?

3. Testimony 3:

   - What was the name of this survivor?

   - What did he/she talk about?

   - What are your thoughts and feelings about this person's experience?

4. **THINKING QUESTION:** Why is it important to hear these testimonies?

Ending Station – Warsaw Ghetto Uprising (DO AS A CLASS)

Method of Research: Watching a video to find and then discuss information

Highest Bloom's Taxonomy Level: Understanding

Note to librarian: The video used in this station has a couple of things to note. A soldier gets shot in the video and there is a very difficult story about a young girl at the end. Discovery Education allows you to edit their videos. I edited these two parts out of the video and showed the edited version to the whole class at the same time. Removing these two parts did not remove the important and meaningful parts of the video I wanted my students to absorb.

Directions:

- As a class watch the video of Warsaw Ghetto Uprising from Discovery Education.
  - ◦ Go to Discovery Education: http://www.discoveryeducation.com
  - ◦ Login with your username and password
  - ◦ Search for "The Warsaw Ghetto Uprising, 1943"
- To be able to understand the whole video, do not answer any questions until the video is over.

Information to Research:

1. What is the woman in this video describing?

2. Was she there during the Warsaw Ghetto Uprising?

3. What were the witness's verbal (speaking) and nonverbal (facial expressions, gestures, etc.) messages? In other words, what did each of these tell us?

4. In a paragraph of at least five complete sentences, write your reactions to this woman's story.

Materials Needed for *Milkweed* Learning Stations

Beginning Station (DO TOGETHER AS A CLASS) – Warsaw Poland – Discovery Education Video

- Discovery Education Video: "Ultimate Survival" – Also found here: http://tinyurl.com/ultsurv (original: http://www.smavideo.com/store/titledetail.cfm?MerchID=30521)

Station 1 – Geography of Warsaw and Berlin – Online World Atlas & Google Earth

- World Atlas Website - http://www.worldatlas.com/aatlas/world.htm
- World Atlas Travel Aid Website - http://www.worldatlas.com/travelaids/travelaids.htm
- Google Earth

Station 2 – Children of the Warsaw Ghetto – Website and Books

- Website: http://tinyurl.com/warsawchildren (original http://resources.ushmm.org/inquery/uia_query.php?noframes=x&page_len=25&max_docs=all&db_group=ushmm&db_name=photos&db_name=wlc&db_name=fvarchive&query_append=type%28photo+or+histphoto+or+instphoto%29&query=warsaw+ghetto+children)
- eBooks that have pictures of the children of the Warsaw Ghetto

Station 3 – Hitler, Himmler, Korczak – Databases and EasyBib

- School subscription databases
- EasyBib

Station 4 – Diseases – Tuberculosis and Typhus – Databases, Website, and EasyBib

- For tuberculosis:
  - School subscription databases
  - Website: http://tinyurl.com/TBarticle (original: http://business.highbeam.com/437850/article-1G1-169434900/tuberculosis
  - Easybib
- For Typhus
  - School subscription databases
  - EasyBib

Station 5 – Testimonies of Warsaw Ghetto Survivors – Website and Videos

- Website: http://tinyurl.com/warsawsurvivors (original: http://resources.ushmm.org/inquery/uia_query.php?noframes=x&page_len=25&max_docs=all&db_group=ushmm&db_name=photos&db_name=wlc&db_name=fvarchive&db_name=website&query=warsaw+ghetto&query_append=type%28testimony%29)
- Headphones
- Headphones sign

Ending Station (DO TOGETHER AS A CLASS) – Warsaw Ghetto Uprising – Discovery Education Video

- **Video** edited from **Discovery Education** of **"Warsaw Ghetto Uprising"** to remove soldier getting shot and little girl story at the end

Rotation Song Suggestion: Something soft, somber and instrumental

Student Pre-Self-Assessment:

These questions are to be answered before the lesson takes place. The questions can be multiple choice for data collection purposes or students may fill in the blank.

1. What is a good source to use for historical research? (If you haven't learned this yet or you don't know, put IDK.)

2. What are two diseases people often contracted while in concentration camps? (If you haven't learned this yet or you don't know, put IDK.)

3. What happened during the Warsaw Ghetto Uprising? (If you haven't learned this yet or you don't know, put IDK.)

4. How far away is Warsaw, Poland, where Milkweed takes place, from Berlin, Germany, which was the headquarters of Nazi Germany? (If you haven't learned this yet or you don't know, put IDK.)

Student Post-Self-Assessment:

These questions are to be answered after the lesson takes place. Any or all of the following questions can be used in an assessment of your choice (see Chapter 6) for this set of multimedia learning stations. The questions can be multiple choice for data collection purposes or students may fill in the blank.

1. What is a good source to use for historical research?

2. What are two diseases people often contracted while in concentration camps?

3. What happened during the Warsaw Ghetto Uprising?

4. How far away is Warsaw, Poland, where Milkweed takes place, from Berlin, Germany, which was the headquarters of Nazi Germany?

5. What is something specific you learned today that surprised you?

6. Complete this sentence. "After today, I am still struggling with..."

7. What learning stations did you find to be the most interesting? Check all that apply.

   • Beginning Station - Warsaw Poland – Discovery Education Video

   • Station 1 - Geography of Warsaw and Berlin - Online World Atlas and Google Earth

   • Station 2 - Children of the Warsaw Ghetto – Website and Books

   • Station 3 - Hitler, Himmler, Korczak – Databases and EasyBib

   • Station 4 - Diseases – Tuberculosis and Typhus – Databases, Website, and EasyBib

   • Station 5 - Testimonies of Warsaw Ghetto Survivors – Website and Videos

   • Ending Station - Warsaw Ghetto Uprising – Discovery Education Video

8. What would you change about your learning process if you were to do these stations again?

9. Overall, how would you assess your learning today?

   • I did extremely well. I learned a lot about my topic and wonder about more. I learned some research skills to use in the future.

   • I did well. I learned something about my topic and how to research in the future.

   • I did OK. I could have worked a little harder, but I learned something about my topic and researching.

   • I wasn't on my game today. I didn't learn nearly as much as I could have.

   • I didn't do anything today, so I didn't learn anything.

10. Kindly list any suggestions you have for improving these stations.

Big Project Assessment Option:

Digital Storytelling

Student Directions:

In Station 2 of the Multimedia Learning Stations for *Milkweed*, you wrote a paragraph in first person from the perspective of one of the children from the Warsaw Ghetto. For this assignment, you are going to expand on that piece of writing, making it longer and telling the story of the child you selected through digital storytelling. This should be historical fiction. You do not need to know the details of who the child is. Your story will be fictional but based in a historic time and place. The information you use in your writing needs to be historically accurate for the time period.

There are two different options for this assignment. You may use one of the two following websites for this assignment:

1. inklewriter - http://www.inklestudios.com/inklewriter/ - a digital storytelling website that allows you to create an interactive "Choose You Own Adventure" story.

2. FlipSnack - http://www.flipsnack.com/ - a digital storytelling website that helps you to create a magazine spread.

Librarian/Teacher Directions: Depending on the age level of the students, more specifics for the assignment length and content will need to be created.

English 4

The Outsiders Learning Stations

Grade Level: 7–9

Subject Standards from Virginia Standards of Learning

English: http://www.doe.virginia.gov/testing/sol/standards_docs/english/index.shtml

7th Grade – 7.6, 7.9
8th Grade – 8.6, 8.9
9th Grade – 9.5, 9.8

AASL Standards

1 - Inquire, think critically, and gain knowledge

- 1.1 Skills – 1.1.2, 1.1.6, 1.1.7, 1.1.8, 1.1.9

- 1.2 Dispositions in Action – 1.2.6, 1.2.7

- 1.3 Responsibilities – 1.3.4, 1.3.5

2 - Draw conclusions, make informed decisions, apply knowledge to new situations, and create new knowledge

- 2.1 Skills – 2.1.3, 2.1.5

- 2.2 Dispositions in Action – 2.2.4

- 2.3 Responsibilities – 2.3.1, 2.3.3

- 2.4 Self-Assessment Strategies – 2.4.1, 2.4.2, 2.4.3, 2.4.4

3 - Share knowledge and participate ethically and productively as members of our democratic society

- 3.1 Skills – 3.1.6

- 3.2 Dispositions in Action – 3.2.1, 3.2.2, 3.2.3

- 3.4 Self-Assessment Strategies – 3.4.1, 3.4.3

Modifications for Special Education Students:

1. Station 2 - Help students understand how to read the prejudice chart, and walk them through how to determine what type of prejudice occurs in *The Outsiders*. Many students automatically say "racism," because that is the only form of prejudice they have studied.

2. Station 5 - Remove

Beginning Station – S. E. Hinton (DO AS A CLASS)

Method of Research: Listening to a video interview for information

Highest Bloom's Taxonomy Level: Understanding

Information to Research:

1. How old was S. E. Hinton when she published *The Outsiders*?

2. What inspired her to write?

3. What grade was she in when she wrote *The Outsiders*?

4. When did she get her contracts?

5. Why does she write from a male point of view?

6. Was she a Soc or a Greaser? To which character did she most relate?

7. How old was her son when he first read *The Outsiders*?

8. Why does she like writing about teenagers?

9. What is S. E. Hinton most proud of?

10. What does she find about writing from a male point of view?

11. Was *The Outsiders* an overnight success (did it become famous right away)?

12. **THINKING QUESTION:** What surprised you in this video interview, and why was it surprising?

Station 1 – Elvis Presley, The Beatles, and Bob Dylan

Method of Research: Searching and reading a website for information

Highest Bloom's Taxonomy Level: Understanding

PLAY Outsiders Playlist on the iPod

Directions:

- Divide the musicians Elvis Presley, the Beatles, and Bob Dylan among your group members. Make sure each musician is being researched by at least one person in your group.
- Go to the website for the Rock and Roll Hall of Fame: http://rockhall.com/.
- In the search box, enter your musician's name.
- Use the search result articles to fill in the chart for the musician you are assigned to research for your group. If you cannot find an answer, you may need to select a different search result.
- Share the information with others in your group, until you have filled in your whole chart.

I tell students they are not allowed to get answers for other sections from their group members until they have completed an entire section on their own. Sharing means giving and taking, not just taking!

Information to Research:

	Elvis Presley	Beatles	Bob Dylan
From...			
Famous song title			
Famous for...			
Touching story from the life of the musician/band (What makes them feel "Human" to you?)			
Is/Are the artist(s) more similar to Greasers or Socs?			

Station 2 – Classism, Prejudice, and Tolerance

Method of Research: Using print or online dictionaries, books, and eBooks to research

Highest Bloom's Taxonomy Level: Analyzing

> **Directions:** Three types of prejudice are listed below. Use a print or an online dictionary to look up each word. Write the definition next to each word.

1. Racism –

2. Ageism –

3. Classism –

> **Directions:** Using the definition of the types of prejudice list above, answer the following THINKING QUESTIONS.

1. What type of prejudice takes place in *The Outsiders*?

2. What groups in *The Outsiders* are prejudiced? Explain your answer.

3. What groups experience others being prejudiced toward them? Explain your answer.

> **Directions:** Use books that cover the topics of *tolerance* and *prejudice*, and use dictionaries to answer the following questions.

Information to Research:

1. What is the meaning of the word "tolerance"?

2. Why is tolerance so important?

3. What is one of the first steps to take in learning to be more tolerant?

4. Define stereotypes, prejudice, and discrimination.
   - Stereotypes -
   - Prejudice -
   - Discrimination -

5. Why does intolerance occur?

6. **THINKING QUESTION:** How can you educate yourself to become more tolerant to others who are not like you?

Station 3 – Drive-ins, Paul Newman, and Cars

Method of Research: Searching and reading websites and Google Images for information

Highest Bloom's Taxonomy Level: Analyzing

Directions: Go to the website http://tinyurl.com/driveinnow to find the answers to the questions below.

Information to Research:

1. What are some things that make a drive-in a better movie option than an indoor multiplex?

2. *The Outsiders* is set in Oklahoma. Click on the link for OKLAHOMA on the right. When did Oklahoma get its start as a venue for outdoor theatres (drive-in movies)?

3. How many drive-in theatres remain open in Oklahoma today?

4. Do you think a drive-in or a multiplex theatre is better to go to for watching a movie and why?

Directions: Do a Google Image search for "Paul Newman" **and** for "Cool Hand Luke"

Information to Research:

1. Describe how Paul Newman looks during the filming of *Cool Hand Luke*.

2. **THINKING QUESTION:** Why do you think Ponyboy likes Paul Newman?

Directions: Go to the website http://tinyurl.com/acorvair to find answers for the questions below.

Information to Research:

1. The Chevy Corvair was a smaller car built with what kind of engine?

2. Under the picture, click on the black arrow in the yellow sign. The Corvair Monza accounted for what percentage of total Corvair sales?

3. **THINKING QUESTION:** Why do you think the Socs like Corvairs?

Directions: Go to following link and select *Convertibles*: http://tinyurl.com/amustang

Information to Research:

1. Name two of the features found on a Mustang convertible.

2. **THINKING QUESTION:** Why do you think the Greasers like Mustangs?

Station 4 – Gangs, Family Violence and Teen Runaways

Method of Research: Searching and reading eBooks for information

Highest Bloom's Taxonomy Level: Creating

Directions: Use ebooks that cover the topics "Gangs," "Teen Runaways," and/or "Family Violence" to answer the questions below.

Information to Research:

1. According to the dictionary, what is the definition of a gang?

2. List at least three reasons young people may join a street gang.

3. How many gangs exist in the United States?

4. Who are most likely to be victims of violence and abuse?

5. What are four different types of abuse?

6. What can a young person do if he/she is experiencing abuse?

7. What are some of the long-term effects of violence suffered by children?

8. Approximately how many runaways are currently living on the streets?

9. What is the most common motive (reason) for kids to run away?

10. What types of centers can help kids get off the streets?

11. **THINKING QUESTION:** What can you point out about gangs, teen runaways, and family violence correlating to each other? How are they connected?

12. **THINKING QUESTION:** How would you improve or help control the problems of gangs, teen runaways, or family violence?

Station 5 – 1960s Flashback

Method of Research: Reading a website for information

Highest Bloom's Taxonomy Level: Understanding

Directions: Go to the website http://tinyurl.com/65flashback to find answers for the questions below.

Information to Research:

1. Who were the president and vice president of the United States in 1965?

2. What was a person's life expectancy (the average number of years that a person may expect to live) in 1965?

3. How much was the average cost of a home in 1965?

4. In the left-hand column, select the link for **Music**. What were the top five songs in 1965, and who recorded them?

5. In the left-hand column, select the link for **TV**. What were the top three T.V. shows in 1965?

6. In the left-hand column, select the link for **Sports**. Who won the NFL (professional football) championship game in 1965 (the Super Bowl didn't get its start until 1967)?

7. Who won the NBA (professional basketball) championship game in 1965?

8. Who won the World Series (professional baseball) in 1965?

Materials Needed for *The Outsiders* Learning Stations

Beginning Station – S. E. Hinton – Video (Watch as a whole class before rotations)

- *Great Women Writers* video: "S. E. Hinton"

Station 1 – Elvis Presley, The Beatles, & Bob Dylan – Website

- Rock and Roll Hall of Fame website: http://rockhall.com

- iPod Touches

- *The Outsiders* playlist put on iPods - Playlist has 30-second clips of the following songs:
    - "Heartbreak Hotel" - Elvis Presley
    - "Jailhouse Rock" - Elvis Presley
    - "Eight Days a Week" - Beatles
    - "Rock and Roll Music" - Beatles
    - "Kansas City" - Beatles
    - "Like a Rolling Stone" - Bob Dylan
- iPod stands
- Belkin Rockstar headphone splitters
- Headphones
- Headphones sign

Station 2 – Classism, Prejudice, & Tolerance – Chart and Book

- Print or online dictionaries
- Books that cover the topics of Prejudice and Tolerance

Station 3 – Drive-ins, Paul Newman, & Cars – Websites

- Drive-in movie website: http://tinyurl.com/driveinnow (original: http://www.driveinmovie.com/mainmenu.htm)

- Corvair website: http://tinyurl.com/acorvair (original: http://corvaircorsa.com/monza.html)

- 1965 Total Performance Mustangs brochure website: http://tinyurl.com/amustang (original: http://www.vintage-mustang.com/topics/brochure/brochure.html)

- Google Images: "Paul Newman" and "Cool Hand Luke"

Station 4 – Gangs, Family Violence and Teen Runaways – Books

- Books that cover Gangs, Family Violence and/or Teen Runaways

Station 5 – 1960s Flashback – Website

- 1960s Flashback website: http://tinyurl.com/65flashback (original: http://www.1960sflashback.com/1965/Economy.asp)

Student Pre-Self-Assessment:

These questions are to be answered before the lesson takes place. The questions can be multiple choice for data collection purposes or students may fill in the blank.

1. What is a good source to use for research? (If you haven't learned this yet or you don't know, put IDK.)

2. Who was a popular musician in the 1960s? (If you haven't learned this yet or you don't know, put IDK.)

3. What type of prejudice occurs in The Outsiders? (If you haven't learned this yet or you don't know, put IDK.)

4. Who is most likely to be abused in this story? (If you haven't learned this yet or you don't know, put IDK.)

Student Post-Self-Assessment:

These questions are to be answered after the lesson takes place. Any or all of the following questions can be used in an assessment of your choice (see Chapter 6) for this set of multimedia learning stations. The questions can be multiple choice for data collection purposes or students may fill in the blank.

1. What is a good source to use for research?

2. Who was a popular musician in the 1960s?

3. What type of prejudice occurs in *The Outsiders*?

4. Who is most likely to be abused?

5. What is something specific you learned today that surprised you?

6. What learning stations did you find to be the most interesting? Check all that apply.

   - Station 1 - Elvis Presley, The Beatles, & Bob Dylan – Website

   - Station 2 - Classism, Prejudice, & Tolerance – Chart and Book

   - Station 3 - Drive-ins, Paul Newman, & Cars – Websites

- Station 4 - Gangs, Family Violence and Teen Runaways - eBooks
- Station 5 - 1960s Flashback - Website

7. What would you change about your learning process if you were to do these stations again?

8. Overall, how would you assess your learning today?

   - I did extremely well. I learned a lot about my topic and would like to learn about more. I learned some research skills to use in the future.

   - I did well. I learned something about my topic and learned some tips on how to research that I can use in the future.

   - I did OK. I could have worked a little harder, but I learned something about my topic and researching.

   - I wasn't on my game today. I didn't learn nearly as much as I could have.

   - I didn't do anything today, so I didn't learn anything.

9. Kindly list any suggestions you have for improving these stations:

Big Project Assessment Option:

Using the research from the library multimedia learning stations on *The Outsiders*, students should create a flipbook using FlipSnack (http://www.flipsnack.com/). The flipbook should be from the point of view of one of the Outsiders or one of the Socs.

The flip book should include at least five images of things the specific character would like. With each image, text should be included, describing what each image is and why their character chose each particular image for their personal flipbook.

English 5

Scorpions Learning Stations

Grade Level: 8–11

Subject Standards from Virginia Standards of Learning

English: http://www.doe.virginia.gov/testing/sol/standards_docs/english/index.shtml

8th Grade – 8.6, 8.9
9th Grade – 9.5, 9.8
10th Grade – 10.5, 10.8
11th Grade – 11.5, 11.8

AASL Standards

1 - Inquire, think critically, and gain knowledge

- 1.1 Skills – 1.1.2, 1.1.6, 1.1.7, 1.1.8, 1.1.9
- 1.2 Dispositions in Action – 1.2.3, 1.2.6, 1.2.7
- 1.3 Responsibilities – 1.3.2, 1.3.4, 1.3.5
- 1.4 Self-Assessment Strategies – 1.4.1, 1.4.2, 1.4.3, 1.4.4

2 - Draw conclusions, make informed decisions, apply knowledge to new situations, and create new knowledge

- 2.1 Skills – 2.1.1, 2.1.2, 2.1.3, 2.1.4, 2.1.5, 2.1.6
- 2.2 Dispositions in Action – 2.2.3, 2.2.4
- 2.3 Responsibilities – 2.3.1, 2.3.2, 2.3.3
- 2.4 Self-Assessment Strategies – 2.4.1, 2.4.2, 2.4.3

3 - Share knowledge and participate ethically and productively as members of our democratic society

- 3.1 Skills – 3.1.1, 3.1.2, 3.1.3, 3.1.4, 3.1.5, 3.1.6
- 3.2 Dispositions in Action – 3.2.1, 3.2.2, 3.2.3
- 3.3 Responsibilities – 3.3.1, 3.3.2, 3.3.3, 3.3.5, 3.3.6
- 3.4 Self-Assessment Strategies – 3.4.1, 3.4.3

Modifications for Special Education Students:

1. Station 1 - Work with students to make sure they understand the concept of gentrification beyond the dictionary definition.

2. Station 2 - Question 3 - Change to list 3, Question 4 - change to one link

3. Station 3 - Make this a double station (set up a duplicate station and have students stay through two rotations). Also, if an extra staff member or volunteer is available, station that person at this station to help. It is a very difficult station, but students can do it with help.

4. Station 4 - Students struggle with the concept that supporting gun control means not supporting (or limiting) gun ownership and opposing gun control means being in support of gun ownership. Make sure they understand these different concepts.

5. These stations will work well spread over two class periods rather than one.

Station 1 – Harlem and Gentrification

Method of Research: Comparing photographs and reading websites to gather information and using Padlet to share information

Highest Bloom's Taxonomy Level: Evaluating

> **Directions:** Go to http://www.google.com. Type "define gentrification" in the search box and hit enter. Write the definition.

Gentrification:

> **Directions:** Look at the pictures on the following link to compare Harlem in the late 1980s to Harlem in 2007: http://tinyurl.com/harlembeforeafter.

1. What are some of the major differences you see?

2. **THINKING QUESTION:** Is this gentrification? Why or why not?

> **Directions:**
> * Go to the following link to record your response on Padlet: http://tinyurl.com/examharlemgentpadlet
> * These answers will be visible to everyone on the Internet, so DO NOT INCLUDE YOUR LAST NAME!

3. On the card on Padlet, please include:

   * First Name and Last INITIAL (NO last names—this is the internet!)

   * Teacher and Period

   * Response

Jen S
Tourje Per. 1
I'm amazed at how destroyed and trashed everything looks in the 1980's and how much nicer it looks in 2007.

> **Directions:** Use the following link from the Gotham Gazette to learn more about the population of Harlem of the last century: http://tinyurl.com/racedataharlem

Information to Research:

4. What do you notice about the race of the population of the people living in Harlem over the decades? Explain the changes you see.

> **Directions:** Use the following links to learn about Harlem's history:
> * http://tinyurl.com/harlemhist
> * http://tinyurl.com/harlem2ndren
> * http://harlemworldmag.com/about/history/

Information to Research:

5. How did Harlem begin?

6. What was the Harlem Renaissance?

7. What was Harlem like in the1930s and 1940s? 1960s? 1980s? 2000s?

   * 1930s and 1940s –

   * 1960s –

   * 1980s –

   * 2000s –

8. Based on the data and information you have collected during this station, what has changed in Harlem since Jamal lived there in the mid- to late-1980s?

Station 2 – Gangs

Method of Research: Watching a video and reading .gov websites for information

Highest Bloom's Taxonomy Level: Create

> **Directions:**
> * Login to Discovery Education (www.discoveryeducation.com)
> * Search for "Gangs"
> * Select "Consequences of Gang Life" (1:57)

Information to Research:

1. What are some consequences of being in a gang?

2. What are some of the hardest personal consequences the former gang members in this video faced?

> **Directions:** Select the following link to get to the United States Department of Justice Toolkit on dealing with gangs: http://tinyurl.com/dojgangstoolkit.

Information to Research:

3. Using the Gangs Toolkit from the link above, determine some of the problems gangs create in a community. List three to five of those reasons.

> **Directions:** Select the following link to go to the Department of Justice's Frequently Asked Questions (FAQ) on gangs: http://tinyurl.com/dojgangsfaq.

Information to Research:

4. Select two of the links that interest you, and summarize the information.

   - Link Name -

   - Summarize -

   - Link Name -

   - Summarize -

5. **THINKING QUESTION:** Devise a way for police to eliminate gangs.

Station 3 – Crime Statistics for Richmond and New York City

Method of Research: Reading websites, charts, and graphs for information

Highest Bloom's Taxonomy Level: Evaluating

> **Directions:** Divide the following topics among your group members then SHARE your data:
> 1. Henrico
> 2. Richmond
> 3. Harlem
> 4. New York City

Information to Research:

If you are researching Henrico_____:

1. Go to the following link to get to the ThingLink: http://tinyurl.com/rvanyccrime

   - Find the link for Henrico Crime Statistics for 2013 and select it

   - Once the document on this link loads, type Henrico in the find box and hit enter until you see Henrico at the TOP of a column (you may have to hit enter three or four times).

   - Make sure you add the adult and juvenile arrests together.

   - Place the data in the chart under **Henrico 2013**

2. Go back to the ThinkLink website and select the FBI's Uniform Crime Reporting Statistics Webpage

   - Under Choose a State, select **Virginia**

   - Select **Next**

   - Under "a. Choose an agency," select **Henrico County Police Dept**

   - Under "b. Choose one or more variable groups," select **Number of violent crimes**

- Under "c. Choose years to include," put **From: 1985 To: 1985**
- Select **Get Table**
- Fill in the chart below under **Henrico 1985**

If you are researching Richmond:

1. Go to the following link to get to the ThingLink: http://tinyurl.com/rvanyccrime
   - Find the links for Richmond Crime Statistics 2013 and select it
   - Once this link loads, click on the picture of the chart
   - Use the data to fill in the chart below.

2. Go back to the ThinkLink website and select the FBI's Uniform Crime Reporting Statistics Webpage
   - Under Choose a State, select **Virginia**
   - Select **Next**
   - Under "a. Choose an agency," select **Richmond (City) Bureau of Police**
   - Under "b. Choose one or more variable groups," select **Number of violent crimes**
   - Under "c. Choose years to include," put **From: 1985 To: 1985**
   - Select **Get Table**
   - Fill in the chart below for **City of Richmond**

If you are researching Harlem:

1. Go to the following link to get to the ThingLink: http://tinyurl.com/rvanyccrime
   - Find the link for Harlem (32nd precinct) Crime Statistics and select it
   - Once the document on this link loads, scroll down to **Historical Perspective**
   - Use the data listed under 2014 and under 1990 to fill in the chart below.

If you are researching New York City:

1. Go to the following link to get to the ThingLink: http://tinyurl.com/rvanyccrime
   - Find the link for New York City Crime Statistics and select it
   - Once the document on this link loads, scroll down to **Historical Perspective**
   - Use the data listed under 2014 under Year to Date to fill in the chart below.

2. Go back to the ThinkLink website and select the FBI's Uniform Crime Reporting Statistics Webpage

	Henrico		City of Richmond		Harlem (32nd Precinct)		New York City	
	1985	2013	1985	2013	1990	2014	1985	2014
Murder/ Homicides								
Robbery								

Directions: Do the rest of this station together as a group. Use the data you gathered and compiled in the chart to answer the questions below. You may discuss your ideas and determine your answers with the group.

Information to Research:

1. What do you notice is different between the crime rates in Henrico and the city of Richmond?

2. What has happened with the numbers of violent crimes in Richmond over the years?

3. What do you notice about the number of murders and overall crimes in the 32nd precinct since 1990?

4. What do you notice about the number of murders and overall crimes in New York City since 1985?

Directions: Looking at all the information from above, answer the following questions:

1. **THINKING QUESTION:** What could have caused the changes in the crime rate over the years?

2. **THINKING QUESTION:** How could you research the reasons for the change?

3. **THINKING QUESTION:** How have New York City and Harlem changed since Jamal lived there in the late 1980s?

Station 4 – Gun Control

Method of Research: Reading databases for information

Highest Bloom's Taxonomy Level: Evaluating

Directions:
- Use the school subscription databases and search for "Gun Control."
- USE MORE THAN ONE ARTICLE to read and gather information.
- YOU WILL CITE ALL THESE SOURCES IN QUESTION NUMBER 4.

Information to Research:

1. What does gun control mean?

2. What are at least three reasons from your research for why people support gun control?

3. What are at least three reasons from your research for why people oppose gun control?

4. Cite your sources here.

Directions: Go to the following link to take a two-question survey on whether you support or oppose gun control: http://tinyurl.com/exguncontrolpoll.

Information to Research:

4. Did you complete the survey?

Station 5 – Technology in the Mid-to-Late 1980s

Method of Research: Reading a websites and comparing images for information

Highest Bloom's Taxonomy Level: Creating

Play the song "Can't Live without My Radio" by LL Cool J

Directions:

A lot of technology was created in the 1980s, the time period *Scorpions* is set in. Many of the devices serve the same purposes as our current devices we use today. Use the following websites to research 1980s technologies and compare them to our technologies now. Put your information in the chart below.

- http://tinyurl.com/80stechnology
- http://tinyurl.com/nprboombox
- http://tinyurl.com/walkmaninvention
- http://tinyurl.com/beeper-pager

Information to Research:

	What is it?	What was it used for in the 1980s?	What device do we use now to serve this purpose?
Boom Box			
Beeper (pager)			
Recording machine (VCR)			
Walkman			

1. **THINKING QUESTION:** What do you think the next big invention will be?

2. **THINKING QUESTION:** What will the purpose of the next big invention be? Will it be used for a purpose a current device serves now, or will it be something with a brand-new purpose?

Materials Needed for *Scorpions* Learning Stations

Station 1 – Harlem & Gentrification – Websites, Padlet, and Google

- Google website - http://www.google.com - "define gentrification"

- Harlem 1980s & 2007 Google Doc - http://tinyurl.com/harlembeforeafter (original: https://docs.google.com/document/d/1Cm5fBiHlcoGLLB2tkhZrvLTc9GV4PW27E7lYlAkDMmk/edit?pli=1)

- Harlem Padlet Example Website - http://tinyurl.com/examharlemgentpadlet (original: http://padlet.com/jenother/tsmodwv1dwf4)

- Harlem's Shifting Population - http://tinyurl.com/racedataharlem (original: http://www.gothamgazette.com/graphics/2008/08/HarlemDemoChart.jpg)

- History of Harlem - http://tinyurl.com/harlemhist (original: http://macaulay.cuny.edu/eportfolios/lobel11 neighborhoods/harlem/history-of-harlem/)

- The Morningside Post: Harlem's Second Renaissance - http://tinyurl.com/harlem2ndren (original: http://www.themorningsidepost.com/2010/11/12/harlems-second-renaissance/)

- History by Harlem World - http://www.harlemworldmag.com/about/history/

Station 2 – Gangs – Discovery Education Video and .Gov Websites

- Discovery Education Video "Consequences of Gang Life" (1:57)

- COPS: Community Oriented Policing Services: Gang Toolkit - http://tinyurl.com/dojgangstoolkit (original: http://www.cops.usdoj.gov/default.asp?item=1309)

- National Gang Center FAQ About Gangs - http://tinyurl.com/dojgangsfaq (original: http://www.nationalgang center.gov/About/FAQ)

- Headphones and headphones sign

Station 3 – Crime Statistics for Richmond and New York City – ThingLink and Websites

- ThingLink with website links: http://tinyurl.com/rvanyccrime (original: http://www.thinglink.com/scene/388743995238383616)

- Henrico - http://www.vsp.state.va.us/downloads/Crime_in_Virginia/Crime_in_Virginia_2013.pdf

- Richmond - http://wtvr.com/2014/11/12/violent-crimes-drop-around-nation-richmond-numbers-remain-high/

- Extra Richmond Info - http://rvanews.com/richmond-homicides-in-13

- Harlem - http://www.nyc.gov/html/nypd/downloads/pdf/crime_statistics/cs032pct.pdf

- New York City - http://www.nyc.gov/html/nypd/downloads/pdf/crime_statistics/cscity.pdf

- FBI's Uniform Crime Reporting Statistics - http://www.ucrdatatool.gov/Search/Crime/Local/JurisbyJuris.cfm

Station 4 – Gun Control – School Subscription Databases and Google Form Survey

- School subscription databases: "Gun Control"

- Google Form Gun Control Survey Example: http://tinyurl.com/exguncontrolpoll

Station 5 – Technology in the Mid-to-Late 1980s – Websites and Images

- How Stuff Works: 12 New Technologies in the 1980s - http://tinyurl.com/80stechnology (original: http://electronics.howstuffworks.com/gadgets/other-gadgets/80s-tech.htm#page=1)

- NPR Music: A Eulogy for the Boom Box - http://tinyurl.com/nprboombox (original: http://www.npr.org/2009/04/22/103363836/a-eulogy-for-the-boombox)

- Backtrack: Greatest Inventions Poll Gives Props to Sony - http://tinyurl.com/walkmaninvention (original: http://cassette-to-cd.baktrack.com/greatest-inventions-poll-gives-props-to-sony-walkman/)

- Pager Definition - http://tinyurl.com/beeper-pager (original: http://searchmobilecomputing.techtarget.com/definition/pager)

- iPod Touch & stand

- Song: "Can't Live Without My Radio" by LL Cool J

- Headphones

- Headphones sign

Student Pre-Self-Assessment:

These questions are to be answered before the lesson takes place. The questions can be multiple choice for data collection purposes or students may fill in the blank.

1. What is a good source to use for research? (If you haven't learned this yet or you don't know, put IDK.)

2. What is gentrification? (If you haven't learned this yet or you don't know, put IDK.)

3. What is gun control? (If you haven't learned this yet or you don't know, put IDK.)

4. How has Harlem changed since the time Jamal lived there in the 1980s? (If you haven't learned this yet or you don't know, put IDK.)

Student Post-Self-Assessment:

These questions are to be answered after the lesson takes place. Any or all of the following questions can be used in an assessment of your choice (see Chapter 6) for this set of multimedia learning stations. The questions can be multiple choice for data collection purposes or students may fill in the blank.

1. What is a good source to use for research?

2. What is gentrification?

3. What is gun control?

4. How has Harlem changed since the time Jamal lived there in the 1980s?

5. What is something specific you learned today that surprised you?

6. Complete this sentence. "After researching today, I am still struggling with…"

7. What learning stations did you find to be the most interesting? Check all that apply.

    - Station 1 - Harlem and Gentrification - Websites, Padlet, and Google

    - Station 2 - Gangs - Discovery Education Video and .Gov Websites

- Station 3 - Crime Statistics for Richmond and New York City - ThingLink and Websites

- Station 4 - Gun Control - Issues and Controversies Database and Google Form Survey

- Station 5 - Technology in the Mid-to-Late 1980s - Websites and Images

8. What would you change about your learning process if you were to do these stations again?

9. Overall, how would you assess your learning today?

   - I did extremely well. I learned a lot about my topic and would like to learn more. I learned some research skills to use in the future.

   - I did well. I learned something about my topic and a few tips on how to research in the future.

   - I did OK. I could have worked a little harder, but I learned something about my topic and researching.

   - I wasn't on my game today. I didn't learn nearly as much as I could have.

   - I didn't do anything today, so I didn't learn anything.

10. Kindly list any suggestions you have for improving these stations.

Big Project Assessment Option:

Students became familiar with "ThingLink" in Station 3. In groups of two to four, students will create their own ThingLink on the topic of gun control. Reliable resources need to be found and linked to the ThingLink they create. The description attached to each link should contain the paraphrased reasons for supporting or opposing gun control that are presented in the article.

History 1

First Five U.S. Presidents Learning Stations

Created in collaboration with Angie Branyon

Grade Level: 6

Subject Standards from Virginia Standards of Learning

History: http://www.doe.virginia.gov/testing/sol/standards_docs/history_socialscience/index.shtml
United States History to 1865: USI.7

AASL Standards

1 - Inquire, think critically, and gain knowledge

- 1.1 Skills – 1.1.3, 1.1.6, 1.1.7, 1.1.8, 1.1.9

- 1.2 Dispositions in Action – 1.2.6

- 1.3 Responsibilities – 1.3.3, 1.3.5

- 1.4 Self-Assessment Strategies – 1.4.1, 1.4.2, 1.4.4

2 - Draw conclusions, make informed decisions, apply knowledge to new situations, and create new knowledge.

- 2.1 Skills – 2.1.2, 2.1.3, 2.1.5

- 2.2 Dispositions in Action – 2.2.4

- 2.4 Self-Assessment Strategies – 2.4.2, 2.4.3, 2.4.4

3 - Share knowledge and participate ethically and productively as members of our democratic society.

- 3.1 Skills – 3.1.1, 3.1.6

- 3.2 Dispositions in Action – 3.2.3

- 3.4 Self-Assessment Strategies – 3.4.1, 3.4.3

Modifications for Special Education Students:

1. Station 1 - Make this a double station (set up a duplicate station and have students stay through two rotations).

2. Station 2 - Remove.

3. Have students regroup and work together in the classroom on a different day to complete the Ending Station.

Station 1 – Trading Cards

Method of Research: Reading a website for information

Highest Bloom's Taxonomy Level: Applying

***Research the same president at every station.**

Information to Research:

1. What are the dates of your president's birth and death?

2. What was his political party?

3. When was his presidential term (meaning, what years did he serve as president)?

4. What are three accomplishments he achieved during his presidency?

*Be sure to take your Presidential Trading Card with you when you leave this station.

Station 2 – Original Political Parties

Method of Research: Searching subscription databases for information

Highest Bloom's Taxonomy Level: Evaluating

Information to Research:

1. Who led the Federalist Party?

2. What U.S. President supported the Federalist Party policies?

3. Who founded the (Democratic-) Republican Party?

4. What did the federalists advocate (support)?

5. What did the democratic-republicans oppose?

6. What did the democratic-republicans want?

7. What groups of people supported the Federalist Party?

8. What groups of people supported the Democratic-Republican Party?

9. When did the Federalist Party stop functioning?

10. **THINKING QUESTION:** Which party did James Monroe support? What data did you use to arrive at that conclusion?

Station 3 – Homes/Plantations

Method of Research: Searching and reading websites for information

Highest Bloom's Taxonomy Level: Analyzing

***Research the same president at every station.**

> **George Washington Directions:** Take a virtual tour of George Washington's home at the official Mt. Vernon website: http://www.mountvernon.org/virtualtour. Use the information found in the text and the pictures you saw to answer the questions.

Information to Research:

1. How long did George Washington live at Mount Vernon?

2. Who oversaw the construction, design, and interior decoration of Mount Vernon?

3. Click through the virtual tour and look through each of the rooms.

4. Which room do you like best, and why?

5. **THINKING QUESTION:** Compare and contrast things you notice about this house and houses of today.

> **John Adams Directions:** Go to the National Park Services' website on the Adams Family home of Peace field, at http://tinyurl.com/peacefield.

Information to Research:

1. What is another name for the main house at Peace field?

2. How long did relatives of the Adams family live in this house?

3. Next to the Old House is the Stone Library. How many books of the Adams does it contain?

4. In today's dollars, how much did John and Abigail Adams pay for the Old House at Peacefield?

5. **THINKING QUESTION:** Compare and contrast things you notice about the Old House and houses of today.

> **Thomas Jefferson Directions:**
> • Go to the Monticello website, the home of Thomas Jefferson: http://explorer.monticello.org/index.html
> • Once this page opens, click on "General House Tour."

Information to Research:

1. How many farms are on Monticello?

2. How many acres of land does Monticello have?

3. Who designed Monticello?

4. Where did he learn about architecture?

5. What was founded by Jefferson in his retirement?

6. **THINKING QUESTION:** Compare and contrast things you notice about Monticello and houses of today.

Information to Research:

1. What did the Madison's use the Drawing room for?

2. What was Dolly Madison's approach to entertaining in the dining room?

3. Why did Madison need two libraries?

4. What was Mr. Madison's room used for?

5. Go to the official Montpelier website at http://tinyurl.com/montmansion.

6. **THINKING QUESTION:** Compare and contrast things you notice about Montpelier and houses of today.

Information to Research:

1. What are some of the original pieces of furniture owned by the Monroes that are still in the house today?

2. When did the Monroes officially live on the property?

3. What was the estate called when the Monroes lived on it?

4. **THINKING QUESTION:** Compare and contrast things you notice about Ashlawn and houses of today.

Station 4 – Presidential Trivia

Method of Research: Searching and reading subscription databases and books for information

Highest Bloom's Taxonomy Level: Analyzing

*Research the same president at every station.

Information to Research:

1. What president are you in charge of researching today?

   _____

2. Question #1:
   Question #2:
   Question #3:

Information to Research:

3. Select two things about your president to tell the class that you and the class may not have known before researching today. (No birthdays, death dates or family members. Be more creative!)

4. Did the two things you chose have to do with the questions you asked, or did you find more interesting things to use while reading?

5. After reading about your president, what conclusions can you draw about how the people of America viewed him as a president?

Station 5 – Historical Documents

Method of Research: Searching subscription databases and websites for information

Highest Bloom's Taxonomy Level: Evaluating

*Research the same president at every station.

> **George Washington Directions:** Go to the following link to answer the questions: http://tinyurl.com/gwfarewelladdress.

Information to Research:

1. Where and when was Washington's Farewell Address published?

2. Washington's Farewell Address was a speech. What is interesting about it?

3. In the Farewell Address, what does Washington set forth as a reason for his leaving the presidency?

4. What are the six major points Washington makes in his Farewell Address?

    1.

    2.

    3.

    4.

    5.

    6.

5. **THINKING QUESTION:** Restate in your own words why George Washington decided to leave the presidency.

> **John Adams Directions:** Use the school subscription databases to research the letters of John and Abigail Adams.

Information to Research:

1. What can we learn about the relationship between John and Abigail Adams through their letters?

2. Who was John Adams biggest political confidante?

3. What made Abigail Adams special and important in politics?

4. John Adams counted on Abigail for many things. What are some of them?

5. **THINKING QUESTION:** What evidence can you find in the letters that lets you see how much John Adams respected his wife Abigail?

> **Thomas Jefferson Directions:**
> • Go to the following link http://tinyurl.com/dofiarchive.
> • Select "Declaration of Independence" to answer the questions.

Information to Research:

1. The Declaration of Independence was drafted (written) by Thomas Jefferson 25 years before he became President. After reading the paragraph on the left-hand side of the webpage, explain from what the colonists were declaring independence from.

2. What was the "mother country?"

   Scroll down to "Learn More About the Declaration" and read the article "The Declaration of Independence: A History."

3. Scroll down to the "Committee of Five" section. What five men were on the committee to create the Declaration of Independence?

4. Read the fourth paragraph under "The Committee of Five." What were the five distinct parts of the Declaration of Independence?

5. **THINKING QUESTION:** Do you agree with what the men were trying to say in the Declaration of Independence?

> **James Madison Directions:** Use the school subscription databases to research James Madison and the U.S. Constitution. Use as many articles on these two topics as you need to answer the questions below.

Information to Research:

1. How long before James Madison became president did he draft the U. S. Constitution?

2. The Constitution Madison drafted formed the federal government that we know today. Why did James Madison and others fear a strong national government, yet form one anyway?

3. What document, passed by the national Congress, governed the states before the Constitution was drafted?

4. What did the Constitution provide for the nation that the Articles of Confederation did not?

5. **THINKING QUESTION:** In your opinion, what is the most important part of the Constitution? Why is it the most important?

> **James Monroe Directions:** Use the school subscription databases to research the Monroe Doctrine. Use as many articles on this topic as you need to answer the questions below.

Information to Research:

1. What is the Monroe Doctrine?

2. What were the four major points of the Monroe Doctrine?

3. Who persuaded Monroe to independently take this step against Europe?

4. **THINKING QUESTION:** Monroe almost announced his policy of noninterference in the Americas jointly with Britain. Why was it wiser for the United States to announce the Monroe Doctrine independently (by themselves) instead?

Everyone Does the "Ending Station" Last

Remain at the last station you completed.

Ending Station – Sharing Presidential information

Task: Creating a graphic organizer of information

Highest Bloom's Taxonomy Level: Remembering

*Research the same president at every station.

Directions:
- Use the school subscription databases or your answers from the previous stations to answer the questions below
- Fill in the graphic organizers for each of the five presidents as a group
- Discuss the details for each president with your group members as you go.

Information to Research:

1. Name of your president - _____

2. Which number president was he (first, second, third, fourth, or fifth)? - _____

3. Dates of his presidential term (meaning during what years was he President) - _____

4. Birth Date _____ Death Date _____

5. Name of the home where he spent his adult life: _____

6. Political Party to which he belonged: _____

7. Three accomplishments he achieved during his presidency: _____ .

Directions:
- Paste a picture of your president to place in the middle square of the graphic organizer found below.
- Fill in your president's name in the middle box as well.
- Fill in the other boxes with the remaining six questions you answered above.

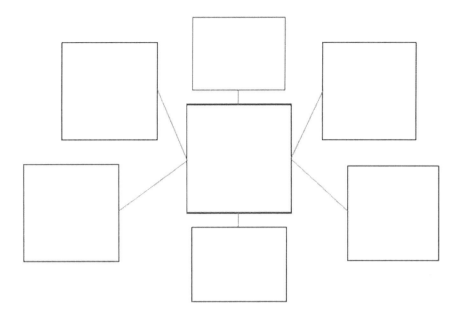

Materials Needed for First Five Presidents Learning Stations

Station 1 – Trading Cards – Website

- Website: http://www.whitehouse.gov/about/presidents/

- Approximately 1½" X 2" pictures of Washington, Adams, Jefferson, Madison, & Monroe – 6 to 7 copies per class period

- Approximately 2" X 3" pieces of Construction Paper – one per student

- Glue sticks

- Pens

Station 2 – Original Political Parties – Databases

- School subscription database articles on Federalist Party and Democratic-Republican Party

Station 3 – Homes/Plantations – Websites and Databases

- Websites for each presidential home:

  ◦ Mount Vernon - http://www.mountvernon.org/virtualtour

  ◦ Peace field - http://tinyurl.com/peacefield (original: http://www.nps.gov/adam/historyculture/places.htm)

- Monticello - http://explorer.monticello.org/index.html

- Montpelier - http://tinyurl.com/jmmontpelierinfo (original: http://www.montpelier.org/research-and-collections/curatorial-collection/furn-pr-house/madison-style)

- Montpelier - http://tinyurl.com/montmansion (original: http://www.montpelier.org/mansion-and-grounds/mansion)

- Ashlawn Highland - http://tinyurl.com/exploreashlawn (original: http://ashlawnhighland.org/plan-your-visit/explore-ashlawn-highland/)

- Ashlawn Highland - http://ashlawnhighland.org/who-we-are/

Station 4 – Presidential Trivia – eBooks and School Subscription Databases

- Books or eBooks on George Washington, John Adams, Thomas Jefferson, James Madison, & James Monroe

- School subscription databases

Station 5 – Historical Documents – Websites and Databases

- Websites:

  - Washington's Farewell Address - http://tinyurl.com/gwfarewelladdress (original: http://www.earlyamerica.com/earlyamerica/milestones/farewell)

  - Declaration of Independence - http://tinyurl.com/dofiarchive (original: http://www.archives.gov/national-archives-experience/charters/declaration.html)

- School subscription databases

Ending Station – Sharing Presidential Information – Previous Sources of Stations 1-5

- Previous sources from stations 1-5

- Previous information researched in stations 1-5

- Graphic organizer for each president

Student Pre-Self-Assessment:

These questions are to be answered before the lesson takes place. The questions can be multiple choice for data collection purposes or students may fill in the blank.

1. What were the first political parties? (If you haven't learned this yet or you don't know, put IDK.)

2. Name the first five presidents in order. (If you haven't learned this yet or you don't know, put IDK.)

3. Name one president and the name of the house he owned. (If you haven't learned this yet or you don't know, put IDK.)

4. List the president who is known for each historical document below. (If you haven't learned this yet or you don't know, put IDK.)

   a. The Monroe Doctrine -

   b. His Farewell Address -

   c. The Declaration of Independence -

   d. The Constitution -

   e. Letters to and from his wife -

5. What is the first resource you use when you are assigned a research topic? (If you haven't studied this before or you don't know, put IDK.)

Student Post-Self-Assessment:

These questions are to be answered after the lesson takes place. Any or all of the following questions can be used in an assessment of your choice (see Chapter 6) for this set of multimedia learning stations. The questions can be multiple choice for data collection purposes or students may fill in the blank.

1. What were the first political parties? (If you haven't learned this yet or you don't know, put IDK.)

2. Name the first five presidents in order. (If you haven't learned this yet or you don't know, put IDK.)

3. Name one president and the name of the house he owned. (If you haven't learned this yet or you don't know, put IDK.)

4. List the president who is known for each historical document below. (If you haven't learned this yet or you don't know, put IDK.)

   a. The Monroe Doctrine -

   b. His Farewell Address -

   c. The Declaration of Independence -

   d. The Constitution -

   e. Letters to and from his wife -

5. What is the most interesting thing you learned about the president you researched today? (No birth or death dates. Be more creative!)

6. What is a good resource to find research?

7. What learning stations did you find to be the most interesting? Check all that apply.

   • Station 1 - Trading Cards - Website

   • Station 2 - Original Political Parties - Subscription Databases

   • Station 3 - Homes/Plantations - Websites

   • Station 4 - Presidential Trivia - Subscription Databases and Books

   • Station 5 - Historical Documents - Subscription Databases and Websites

8. What would you change about your learning process if you were to do these stations again?

9. Overall, how would you assess your learning today?

   • I did extremely well. I learned a lot about my topic and would like to learn more. I learned some research skills to use in the future.

- I did well. I learned something about my topic and some tips on how to research that I can use in the future.

- I did OK. I could have worked a little harder, but I learned something about my topic and researching.

- I wasn't on my game today. I didn't learn nearly as much as I could have.

- I didn't do anything today, so I didn't learn anything.

10. Kindly list any suggestions you have for improving these stations:

Big Project Assessment Option:

Group members should reconvene in the classroom during the next class period. Using Google Presentation, students can all work on the same slide show simultaneously using Google Accounts.

Each student should create two slides on the president they researched in the library while doing multimedia learning stations. The finished product will be a group slide presentation. Group members will be in charge of using their slides to teach the other group members about the presidents they didn't yet research. The final presentations could be presented orally to the class.

History 2

Harlem Renaissance Learning Stations

Grade Level: 7–9

Subject Standards from Virginia Standards of Learning

History: http://www.doe.virginia.gov/testing/sol/standards_docs/history_socialscience/index.shtml
United States History: 1865 to that Present: USII.6

AASL Standards

1. Inquire, think critically, and gain knowledge

    *   1.1 Skills – 1.1.4, 1.1.6, 1.1.7, 1.1.8, 1.1.9

    *   1.2 Dispositions in Action – 1.2.2, 1.2.6

    *   1.3 Responsibilities – 1.3.3, 1.3.5

    *   1.4 Self-Assessment Strategies – 1.4.1, 1.4.2, 1.4.4

2. Draw conclusions, make informed decisions, apply knowledge to new situations, and create new knowledge

    *   2.1 Skills – 2.1.2, 2.1.3, 2.1.4, 2.1.5

    *   2.2 Dispositions in Action – 2.2.3

    *   2.4 Self-Assessment Strategies – 2.4.2, 2.4.3, 2.4.4

3. Share knowledge and participate ethically and productively as members of our democratic society

    *   3.1 Skills – 3.1.3, 3.1.6

    *   3.2 Dispositions in Action – 3.2.3

    *   3.4 Self-Assessment Strategies – 3.4.1, 3.4.3

Modifications for Special Education Students:

1. Station 2 - Explain to students that on the chart, you want them to tell you what made them more memorable than all the other musicians out there who were singing, playing instruments, and leading bands. Why do we study them specifically instead of all the other musicians of the same time period? What makes these musicians special?

2. Spread these learning stations over two days to allow for extra time.

Station 1 – Literature and Art – Langston Hughes and Jacob Lawrence

Method of Research: Reading a website and listening to a podcast for information

Highest Bloom's Taxonomy Level: Analyzing

> **Part I Directions:**
> *   Go to the link http://tinyurl.com/hrjacob
> *   Select "Meet Jacob Lawrence"
> *   In the left-hand column, select "His Harlem Community"
> *   Use the Find function (usually Control-F or Apple-F) on your computer to search for the underlined keywords in each question below

Information to Research:

1. From where did Jacob Lawrence find <u>inspiration</u> for his paintings?

2. What does his early work <u>depict</u> (show)?

3. What were the <u>1930s</u> like for Lawrence? What were they like for his parent's generation?

4. What <u>style</u> of artwork did Jacob Lawrence develop during his early twenties?

5. Jacob Lawrence met many notable writers and activists such as Langston Hughes during the Harlem Renaissance. What did these people <u>emphasize</u>?

Directions: In the left-hand column, select "Visions of Harlem."

Information to Research:

1. What kinds of things in Harlem sparked Jacob Lawrence's imagination?

2. What did Jacob Lawrence emphasize throughout his career?

Directions: At the top of the page, select "Jacob Lawrence's Art."

Information to Research:

1. Select (click onto) your favorite piece of Lawrence's artwork. What is the title of this painting?

2. Why is the painting you selected your favorite painting by Jacob Lawrence?

Part II Directions:
- Go to the link http://tinyurl.com/hrlangston
- Select Listen
- Use the information in the podcast to answer the following questions
- Pause as you go to answer the questions

Information to Research:

1. Langston Hughes's writing flowed with rhythms of what?

2. He was one of the leading figures of what?

3. His writing had an impact on what?

4. When did Langston Hughes die?

5. Who did Langston Hughes claim his poetry was concerned with?

6. What poem is being read, and who is reading it?

7. **THINKING QUESTION:** What do you feel the overall tone of the poem is?

8. **THINKING QUESTION:** Why do you think Langston Hughes is the most famous poet from the Harlem Renaissance?

Station 2 – Music & Theatre – Duke Ellington, Louis Armstrong, and Bessie Smith

Method of Research: Searching for a reading subscription databases to find information

Highest Bloom's Taxonomy Level: Analyzing

Directions:
- Divide the following three musicians among your group members. Make sure each musician is being researched: Duke Ellington, Louis Armstrong, and Bessie Smith
- Use the school subscription databases to search for articles of information
- Use the database articles to fill in the chart for the musician you are assigned to research for your group. If you cannot find an answer, you may need to select a different article.
- Share the information with others in your group, until you have filled in your whole chart.

I tell students they are not allowed to get answers for other sections of the chart from their group members until they have completed an entire section on their own. Sharing means giving *and* taking, not just taking!

Information to Research:

REMEMBER TO DIVIDE THESE MUSICIANS AMONG YOUR GROUP MEMBERS!

Directions: Cite your source. You may find it at the bottom of the database article you used, or you can create an MLA citation using EasyBib (http://www.easybib.com).

MLA Citation:

Musician	What was his or her lifespan? (Birth year through death year)	How long did he or she live? (Age upon death)	What instrument did he or she play? (Voice can be an instrument.)	Why is this musician more famous than other musicians who played the same instrument during the Harlem Renaissance?
Duke Ellington				
Louis Armstrong				
Bessie Smith				

Station 2: Fill in the Chart with the Information You Find

Station 3 – The Jazz Age

Method of Research: Searching a video and listening for information

Highest Bloom's Taxonomy Level: Analyzing

Directions:
- Login to Discovery Education
- Search for and play "Birth of Jazz"
- Play the video and use the information to answer the following questions

Information to Research:

1. What kind of changes were taking place in the 1920s?

2. Where did the Jazz Age start?

3. One of the greatest contributions made to American culture in the 1920s was _____.

4. What coronet player/ bandleader, composer, and singer helped create and refine jazz?

5. The popularity of what helped elevate African American status? Did their rights improve?

6. What movement in the 1920s included not only music, but literature and politics, too?

7. What writer helped introduce African American culture and concerns to the world?

8. Marcus Garvey believed in race pride, and felt African Americans should form a new nation in _____.

9. What marked the first time African American culture and music made its way into popular culture?

10. This was the first time that what happened?

11. **THINKING QUESTION:** Explain the significance of the information in your answers to the last two questions.

Station 4 – Night/Social Life

Method of Research: Searching and reading subscription databases and websites for information

Highest Bloom's Taxonomy Level: Analyzing

Directions: Divide the following three topics among your group: Apollo Theatre, Rent Parties, and Cotton Club. Make sure each topic is being researched by at least one person. Then share your answers with each other to complete all three sections. Each group member must complete a section on his/her own before sharing.

Directions for Apollo Theatre:
- Use the school subscription databases to research "Apollo Theatre."
- Use the articles to find the answers to the questions below.

Information to Research:

1. When was the Apollo Theatre built, and where was it located?

2. What is the Apollo Theatre known for?

3. Name at least three singers who became known after singing at the Apollo.

4. **THINKING QUESTION:** Why was the Apollo Theatre important in the growth of the Harlem Renaissance?

Information to Research:

1. What became the backbone of Harlem nightlife in the 1920s and 1930s?

2. How much did it cost for admission to a rent party?

3. Other than to have fun, why would someone have a rent party?

4. What were wages for African Americans like in New York, and what was rent in Harlem like?

5. How did a host prepare for a rent party?

6. **THINKING QUESTION:** Explain why it was or wasn't easy for African Americans to pay rent in Harlem.

Information to Research:

1. What was the Cotton Club?

2. Who became famous while performing there?

3. Who bought the club in 1922?

4. Who was allowed to be a customer/patron? Who were the entertainers and wait staff?

5. **THINKING QUESTION:** Look at the answers to the previous question. Explain why you think this division existed.

Station 5 – History of the Harlem Renaissance

Method of Research: Searching and listening to a video for information

Highest Bloom's Taxonomy Level: Understanding

Information to Research:

1. Who founded Harlem?

2. A century later who was living in Harlem?

3. Now, Harlem is rich in African American heritage because of what?

4. What does "renaissance" mean?

5. What did the Harlem Renaissance celebrate, and when did the Harlem Renaissance take place?

6. What caused the Harlem Renaissance?

7. Give at least two reasons for why so many African Americans migrated from the South to the North?

8. After the home prices in Harlem dropped, what were many African Americans able to do for the first time?

9. What were common themes of the work from the Harlem Renaissance?

10. What was an even stronger theme of work from the Harlem Renaissance?

11. Even though they weren't in the South, there was still a lot of what during this time in Harlem?

12. Who was much more joyful in his writing than Claude McKay and others from the West Indies?

13. What transformed music during the Harlem Renaissance and who emerged with their own unique styles?

14. The movement of _____ spread throughout the country.

15. What contributed to the end (or decline) of the Harlem Renaissance in the 1930s?

16. The Harlem Renaissance has a lasting impact on African American culture and _____ as a whole?

17. **THINKING QUESTION:** Summarize the information you learned in the video in three sentences.

Materials Needed for Harlem Renaissance Learning Stations

Station 1 – Literature and Art: Langston Hughes and Jacob Lawrence

Podcast and Website

• Jacob Lawrence Exploring Stories webpage—http://tinyurl.com/hrjacob (original: http://whitney.org/www/jacoblawrence/index.html)

• NPR: "Langton Hughes" podcast—http://tinyurl.com/hrlangston (original: http://www.npr.org/templates/story/story.php?storyId=1137068)

• Headphones

• Headphones sign

• Wordle examples constructed with the words in the standards for Jacob Lawrence and Langston Hughes (found on page 140)—http://www.wordle.net/

• Pictures of Jacob Lawrence and his artwork from the Library of Congress Website

• Pictures of Langston Hughes and his drafts of "Ballad of Booker T" from the Library of Congress Website

• Poster board for visuals

Station 2 – Musicians: Duke Ellington, Louis Armstrong, and Bessie Smith - Databases

• School subscription databases

• Wordle examples constructed with the words in the standards for Duke Ellington, Louis Armstrong, and Bessie Smith (found on pages 140 and 141)—http://www.wordle.net/

- Pictures of Duke Ellington and his orchestra list from the Library of Congress Website

- Pictures of Louis Armstrong and Bessie Smith from the Library of Congress Website

- Poster board for visuals

Station 3 – The Jazz Age – Video

- Discovery Education Video: "Birth of Jazz"

- Headphones

- Headphones sign

Station 4 – Night & Social Life – Databases & Websites

- School subscription databases

- Encyclopedia of the Harlem Renaissance: House-Rent Parties website— http://tinyurl.com/rentparties (original: http://cw.routledge.com/ref/harlem/parties.html)

Station 5 – History of the Harlem Renaissance – Video

- Discovery Education Video "The Harlem Renaissance" (6:40)

- Headphones

- Headphones sign

- Wordle examples constructed with the words in the standards for Harlem Renaissance (found on page 141)— http://www.wordle.net/

Rotation Song Suggestions: Songs by Louis Armstrong, Duke Ellington, and Bessie Smith (the Ken Burns Jazz collection has a really good compilation of songs by all three artists)

Student Pre-Self-Assessment:

These questions are to be answered before the lesson takes place. The questions can be multiple choice for data collection purposes or students may fill in the blank.

1. What is a good source to use for historical research? (If you haven't learned this yet or you don't know, put IDK.)

2. What was the Harlem Renaissance? (If you haven't learned this yet or you don't know, put IDK.)

3. Name three famous artist, writers or musicians from the Harlem Renaissance. (If you haven't learned this yet or you don't know, put IDK.)

4. Where did people go for entertainment during the Harlem Renaissance and what would they see there? (If you haven't learned this yet or you don't know, put IDK.)

Student Post-Self-Assessment:

These questions are to be answered after the lesson takes place. Any or all of the following questions can be used in an assessment of your choice (see Chapter 6) for this set of multimedia learning stations. The questions can be multiple choice for data collection purposes or students may fill in the blank.

1. What is a good source to use for historical research?

2. What was the Harlem Renaissance?

3. Name three famous artist, writers or musicians from the Harlem Renaissance.

4. Where did people go for entertainment during the Harlem Renaissance and what would they see there?

5. What is something specific you learned today that surprised you?

6. Complete this sentence. "After today, I am still struggling with…"

7. What learning stations did you find to be the most interesting? Check all that apply:

   • Station 1 - Literature and Art: Langston Hughes and Jacob Lawrence – Podcast and Website

   • Station 2 - Musicians: Duke Ellington, Louis Armstrong, and Bessie Smith - Databases

   • Station 3 - The Jazz Age - Video

   • Station 4 - Night and Social Life – Databases & Websites

   • Station 5 - History of the Harlem Renaissance - Video

8. What would you change about your learning process if you were to do these stations again?

9. Overall, how would you assess your learning today?

   • I did extremely well. I learned a lot about my topic and wonder about more. I learned some research skills to use in the future.

   • I did well. I learned something about my topic and how to research in the future.

   • I did OK. I could have worked a little harder, but I learned something about my topic and researching.

   • I wasn't on my game today. I didn't learn nearly as much as I could have.

   • I didn't do anything today, so I didn't learn anything.

10. Kindly list any suggestions you have for improving these stations.

Big Project Assessment Option:

Students can use the research they gathered during the library multimedia stations to create a publicity poster for Langston Hughes, Jacob Lawrence, Duke Ellington, Louis Armstrong, or Bessie Smith. The flyer or poster should include information about who the person is, where they will be, and some information about the person that would be enticing to the viewer. The completed flyers can also be posted online through a classroom website.

Students may choose between two websites to create this flyer or poster:

Canva - https://www.canva.com/

Smore - https://www.smore.com/

Wordle Examples

Jacob Lawrence Wordle

Langston Hughes Wordle

Duke Ellington Wordle

Louis Armstrong Wordle

Bessie Smith Wordle

Harlem Renaissance Wordle

History 3

Immigration Learning Stations

Grade Level: 7

Subject Standards from Virginia Standards of Learning

History: http://www.doe.virginia.gov/testing/sol/standards_docs/history_socialscience/index.shtml
United States History: 1865 to that Present: USII.4

AASL Standards

1. Inquire, think critically, and gain knowledge
   - 1.1 Skills – 1.1.1, 1.1.2, 1.1.4, 1.1.6, 1.1.7, 1.1.8, 1.1.9
   - 1.2 Dispositions in Action – 1.2.1, 1.2.6, 1.2.7
   - 1.3 Responsibilities – 1.3.2, 1.3.4, 1.3.5
   - 1.4 Self-Assessment Strategies – 1.4.1, 1.4.2, 1.4.3, 1.4.4

2. Draw conclusions, make informed decisions, apply knowledge to new situations, and create new knowledge
   - 2.1 Skills – 2.1.1, 2.1.2, 2.1.3, 2.1.4, 2.1.5
   - 2.2 Dispositions in Action – 2.2.2, 2.2.3
   - 2.4 Self-Assessment Strategies – 2.4.2, 2.4.3, 2.4.4

3. Share knowledge and participate ethically and productively as members of our democratic society
   - 3.1 Skills – 3.1.1, 3.1.2, 3.1.3, 3.1.6
   - 3.2 Dispositions in Action – 3.2.1, 3.2.2, 3.2.3
   - 3.4 Self-Assessment Strategies – 3.4.1, 3.4.3

Modifications for Special Education Students:

1. Station 1 - Help students read and analyze the chart. They often have difficulty determining the difference between sections of the chart. Often the colors or shapes indicating a certain country are too similar for them to differentiate between. They also have a hard time understanding that the push and pull factors listed under the chart correspond with the years in the chart above. Work through this station with students.

2. Station 3 - Have an adult facilitate this discussion. If a regular education and a special education teacher are available, station one of them here. If not, station the teacher or librarian here.

3. Station 6 - Once students have finished placing the events on the timeline, the librarian or the teacher needs to facilitate the discussion of cause and effect of the world events.

Station 1 – Reasons for Immigration

Method of Research: Analyzing a chart on a website for information

Highest Bloom's Taxonomy Level: Understanding

Part 1: There were many events outside of America that were pushing people to immigrate to America from their home countries. This is called PUSH.

Information to Research:

1. Between the years of 1881 and 1930, what were some of the factors that were *pushing* people out of their home countries?

    - Europe –

    - Poland –

    - Russia –

    - Mexico –

    - Canada –

    - Germany, Italy, and Spain –

2. **THINKING QUESTION:** Why would these factors push people out of their home countries?

Part 2: There were also trends and events in America that were pulling people toward the United States and away from their home countries. This is called PULL.

Directions: Using the same chart as Part 1, look closely to find the area with the years between 1881 and 1930. Use only the part of the chart with those years.

Information to Research:

Between the years 1881 and 1930, what were two of the positive factors that would *pull* people toward America? And why would these factors pull immigrants to the United States instead of another country?

    - Positive Pull Factor #1 - _____

    - Why would this pull immigrants to the U.S.?

    - Positive Pull Factor #2 - _____

    - Why would this pull immigrants to the U.S.?

Part 3: During certain years immigrants from specific countries or areas began moving to the United States.

Directions: Use the same chart as Part I to answer the questions below.

Information to Research:

1. Look **only** at the years given below, and determine from where most immigrants were coming between the years listed:

    - 1881-1890 -

    - 1891-1900 -

- 1901-1910 -
- 1911-1920 -
- 1921-1930 -

2. **THINKING QUESTION:** Pick one of the immigrant groups from above. Why would this group of immigrants be coming to the United States in large numbers during the specific years listed?

Station 2 – Immigrant Journey

Method of Research: Exploring an interactive website to understand information

Highest Level of Bloom's Taxonomy: Evaluating

Directions:
- Take an interactive Immigrant Journey by selecting this link: http://tinyurl.com/ellisislandjourney.
- Under the picture, select **Continue** to start your immigrant journey.
- Read the passages, look at the pictures, and select the links to go on a journey.
- Use this information to answer the questions below. Each person who goes on this journey has a different outcome.

Information to Research:

1. What happened to you when you arrived on Ellis Island?

2. What is something you learned about Ellis Island from your journey?

3. What is something that surprised you on your journey?

4. What is your opinion of the way immigrants entered into the United States through Ellis Island?

5. Discuss with your group the questions and your answers to the above questions. You may add more ideas in the discussion as they arise.

Station 3 – Rural to Urban Migration

Method of Research: Using images from Google Earth to conceptualize communities and discuss migration from rural to urban communities

Highest Level of Bloom's Taxonomy: Analyzing

Directions: Look at the images of rural, suburban, and urban areas to help you answer these THINKING QUESTIONS. The answers to the questions will not be written down on the images. You need to discuss the topics together as a group to decide on the answers. You librarian or teacher will be by to help facilitate the discussion.

Information to Discuss:

1. Look at the Google Earth images of rural, urban, and suburban areas. What is another word for:
   - Rural -
   - Urban -
   - Suburban -

2. Since suburban areas didn't exist in the early 1900s, when your group looks at the Google Earth images of rural and urban areas, why do you think immigrants would have moved from a rural area to an urban area?

3. Based on what you see in the Google Earth images of rural and urban areas, what do you think would be easier for immigrants living in urban areas in the early 1900s?

4. Based on what you see in the Google Earth images of rural and urban areas, what do you think would be more difficult for immigrants living in urban areas in the early 1900s?

5. Looking at the Google Earth image of an urban community. Discuss with your group the large quantities of additional people moving into the cities, and how they would be housed. As the population increased in urban areas and the cities grew larger, what types of buildings do you think were invented and began to be built in order to house everyone? (Do not name the purpose of the interior of the building as in apartments or tenements, but name the outside structure of the building.)

6. How would these buildings help with the population growth?

7. How would these types of buildings help create jobs for the many immigrants coming to cities in the United States?

8. Use Google Earth to search for your address or the school address. Look at the image and community. Do you live in a rural, suburban, or urban community?

Station 4 – Immigrant Life

Method of Research: Playing an immigration game and creating a passport and life to understand an immigrant's life

Highest Level of Bloom's Taxonomy: Creating

> **Directions:**
> - Use the Tenement.org website: http://www.tenement.org
> - Play the "Immigration Game"
> - Select the building to enter the website
> - Watch the video and answer the question below

Information to Research:

How many immigrants moved to America between 1890 and 1924?

> **Directions: Become an Immigrant**
> - After the movie, click onto the red hand that says, "Make Your Immigrant Life" (it is on the right-hand side).
> - Follow the directions to make a passport
> - Click on the red hand that says, "Select Your Belongings."
> - Follow the directions and watch the videos of Victoria as you go.

Information to Research:

1. Write at least three things you learned about what an immigrant's experience was like from 1890–1924.

2. How difficult would it be for you and your family to live in a tenement like Victoria's?

Station 5 – Settlement Houses – Jane Addams

Method of Research: Searching subscription online databases for information

Highest Level of Bloom's Taxonomy: Analyzing

> ### Directions:
> - Search for "Settlement Houses" in the school subscription databases.
> - If you don't find the answers in one article, look in another.

Information to Research:

1. What was a settlement house?

2. Why were they called settlement houses?

3. What services did Hull House and other settlement houses provide to immigrants?

4. What did the founders of Hull House and other settlement houses do to promote social reform?

5. **THINKING QUESTION:** In addition to help improving immigrants' lives, how would settlement houses have benefited the whole community?

> ### Directions:
> - Search for "Jane Addams" in the school subscription databases.
> - If you don't find the answers in one article, look in another.

Information to Research:

1. How was Jane Addams inspired to create Hull House?

2. Which other organizations did Jane Addams help found?

3. How did the people in Hull House's neighborhood feel about it at first, and how did that change?

4. At the time of Addams' death in 1935, how big was Hull House?

5. **THINKING QUESTION:** Why is Jane Addams an historical figure who is studied in schools today?

Station 6 – World Events Affecting Immigration

Method of Research: Reading eBooks and books and using prior knowledge to complete a timeline of immigration

Highest Level of Bloom's Taxonomy: Analyzing

> ### Directions:
> - Open the envelope of events concerning immigrants from U.S. History. See if you can correctly place the missing events on the timeline on the floor.
> - You may use the Timelines found in the books in immigration to help
> - After you have placed your events on the timeline, your teacher or librarian will come around to discuss the events on the timeline and help you make connections between the world events and the trends in immigration.

Information to Research:

What are some of the connections you noticed?

Materials Needed for Immigration Learning Stations

Station 1 – Reasons for Immigration – Website with Push/ Pull Charts

- Push/ Pull Charts - http://tinyurl.com/pushpullchart (original: http://www.jaha.org/edu/discovery_center/push -pull/chart_w_events.html)

Station 2 – Immigrant Journey – Website

- Immigrant Journey Interactive Website: http://tinyurl.com/ellisislandjourney (original: http://s55831.gridserver .com/journey/)

Station 3 – Rural to Urban Migration – Images & Google Earth

- Google Earth
- Images from Google Earth of urban, rural, & suburban areas (if possible, use images near where students live)

Station 4 – Immigrant Life – Website & Video

- Tenement.org website http://www.tenement.org to play the "Immigration Game"
- Headphones
- Headphones sign

Station 5 – Settlement Houses & Jane Addams – Subscription Databases

- School subscription databases

Station 6 – World Events Affecting Immigration – Books, eBooks, and Timeline

- Giant floor timeline with some world events already on it
- Books and eBooks on specific immigrant groups coming to America between 1840-1920
- Envelope of World Events - cut up and ready to place on timeline

Rotation Song Suggestion: "America" by Neil Diamond

World Events to include on timeline:

1845   Irish Potato Famine begins
1848   German Revolution fails
1848   Gold Rush begins
1849
1854
1861   Civil War begins
1862   Homestead Act passes allowing people to claim land out west
1862
1865   Building of the Transcontinental Railroad begins – many immigrants get jobs building it
1880
1882
1891   Bad weather ruins grain crops in Russia – 1st time
1892   Ellis Island opens
1892   The beginning of a 20-year surge of 3 million Polish immigrants entering the U.S.
1909   Bad weather ruins grain crops in Russia – 2nd time
1910   Angel Island opens
1914   World War I begins
1917   Russian Revolution
1918
1918   Poland regains its independence
1920

Events to cut up and separate for students to place on timeline:
(Years in parenthesis are the key - students should not be given the years)

Gold Rush draws many Irish immigrants to California (1849)
Over 200,000 Germans emigrate to the U.S. (1854)
Many German immigrants move West (1862)
Biggest group of Italian immigrants leaves Italy for America (1880)
250,000 German immigrants enter the U.S. (1882)
Waves of wealthy, educated Russians arrive in the U.S. (1918)
More than 400,000 Polish immigrants are living in Chicago (1920)

Student Pre-Self-Assessment:

These questions are to be answered before the lesson takes place. The questions can be multiple choice for data collection purposes or students may fill in the blank.

1. What is a good source to use for historical research? (If you haven't learned this yet or you don't know, put IDK.)

2. Describe an immigrant experience of moving to the United States. (If you haven't learned this yet or you don't know, put IDK.)

3. Why would immigrants have moved from rural to urban areas in the early 1900s? (If you haven't learned this yet or you don't know, put IDK.)

4. What were some factors that pushed people out of their countries and others that pulled them to the United States? (If you haven't learned this yet or you don't know, put IDK.)

Student Post-Self-Assessment:

These questions are to be answered after the lesson takes place. Any or all of the following questions can be used in an assessment of your choice (see Chapter 6) for this set of multimedia learning stations. The questions can be multiple choice for data collection purposes or students may fill in the blank.

1. What is a good source to use for historical research?

2. Describe an immigrant experience of moving to the United States.

3. Why would immigrants have moved from rural to urban areas in the early 1900s?

4. What were some factors that pushed people out of their countries, and others that pulled them to the United States?

5. What is something specific you learned today that surprised you?

6. What learning stations did you find to be the most interesting? Check all that apply:
   - Station 1 - Reasons for Immigration – Website with Push/ Pull Charts
   - Station 2 - Immigrant Journey - Website
   - Station 3 - Rural to Urban Migration – Images and Google Earth
   - Station 4 - Immigrant Life – Website and Video
   - Station 5 - Settlement Houses and Jane Addams – Subscription Databases
   - Station 6 - World Events Affecting Immigration – Books, eBooks, and Timeline

7. What would you change about your learning process if you were to do these stations again?

8. Overall, how would you assess your learning today?
   - I did extremely well. I learned a lot about my topic and would like to learn more. I learned some research skills to use in the future.
   - I did well. I learned something about my topic and learned some tips on how to research that I can use in the future.
   - I did OK. I could have worked a little harder, but I learned something about my topic and researching.
   - I wasn't on my game today. I didn't learn nearly as much as I could have.
   - I didn't do anything today, so I didn't learn anything.

9. Kindly list any suggestions you have for improving these stations.

Big Project Assessment Option:

Students can expand on the discussion topics in **Station 3: Rural to Urban Migration** and/or **Station 6: World Events Affecting Immigration** by creating a VoiceThread (http://voicethread.com/).

The librarian can create a VoiceThread using the images from these stations and an overall discussion question. All students would need to comment on the VoiceThread with their respective thoughts, and be a part of the virtual discussion. All comments should be based on evidence gathered from these stations, or they should show sound reasoning for their speculation.

Math 1

Fractions Learning Stations

Grade Level: 6

Subject Standards from Virginia Standards of Learning

Mathematics: http://www.doe.virginia.gov/testing/sol/standards_docs/mathematics/index.shtml

6th Grade: 6.2, 6.7

AASL Standards

1 - Inquire, think critically, and gain knowledge

- 1.1 Skills – 1.1.1, 1.1.2, 1.1.6, 1.1.7, 1.1.8, 1.1.9
- 1.2 Dispositions in Action – 1.2.6
- 1.3 Responsibilities – 1.3.5

2 - Draw conclusions, make informed decisions, apply knowledge to new situations, and create new knowledge

- 2.1 Skills – 2.1.1, 2.1.2, 2.1.3, 2.1.5, 2.1.6
- 2.2 Dispositions in Action – 2.2.3, 2.2.4
- 2.3 Responsibilities – 2.3.1
- 2.4 Self-Assessment Strategies – 2.4.2, 2.4.3, 2.4.4

3 - Share knowledge and participate ethically and productively as members of our democratic society

- 3.2 Dispositions in Action – 3.2.1, 3.2.2, 3.2.3
- 3.4 Self-Assessment Strategies – 3.4.1, 3.4.3

Modifications for Special Education Students:

1. A different recipe can be used for Station 1.
2. The number of learning stations conducted for this topic may change depending on the level of students participating. Station 3 can be removed for time and the song that goes with the video at that station can be played as a rotating song instead. It is a rap called "Fractions" by Mr. Duey, which is surprisingly good.

Important Notes about the Lesson:

- Stations 4 and 5 are combined. Students stay at that learning station for two rotations. Due to this, an area large enough to hold two groups should be dedicated to Stations 4 and 5.

- In order to keep the rotation moving with a double set of learning stations, it is best to have only one group start at 4 and 5. When it's time to rotate, they will stay, but the next group will also rotate there. So, two groups will be there at the same time. At the next rotation, the first group rotates to Station 6 and the third group joins in with the second group at Stations 4 and 5.

- Due to the calculations required of students at learning stations 1, 4, and 5, the librarian and teacher should constantly be working with those stations.

- Parent volunteers, if available, are helpful during this set of multimedia learning stations as well.

Station 1 – Adding Mixed Numeral Fractions and Unlike Denominators

Method of Research: Searching subscription databases for information

Highest Bloom's Taxonomy Level: Evaluating

> **Directions:**
> - With your group, use the Gale Health Reference Center Academic to find the article "Having our cake and eating it with you" OR go to http://tinyurl.com/havingourcake
> - Look at the recipe for the cupcakes (NOT THE FROSTING) to answer the following questions.
> - Calculators may be used

Information to Research:

1. Fill in the chart for the ingredients that go in just the cupcakes:
   - Leave out any ingredient smaller than 1 teaspoon. (Hint: That will leave 8 ingredients)
   - Then write/type **all** 8 ingredients for the cupcakes in cups.
   - Use the Cooking Conversion Chart to convert any tablespoons and teaspoons in your recipe to cups. (E.g., 2 tsp = $\frac{2}{48}$ cups, $\frac{1}{3}$ cup = $\frac{1}{3}$ cup)
   - *Note: 1 egg = $\frac{1}{4}$ cup

Original Ingredients	Amount converted to cups
Ex. ½ cup brown sugar	Ex. ½ cup
Ex. 4 tbs. butter	Ex. ¼ cup
1.	
2.	
3.	
4.	
5.	
6.	
7.	
8.	

2. Combine the like terms in the chart above (or on paper), and type or write an addition problem (**not** the answer) to show how you would add the amounts of the ingredients in cups. Remember to combine like terms first!

3. Find the common denominators for the fraction addition problem in #2 and add the fractions together.

4. How many cups will you use for your recipe?

5. Which bowl most closely fits this measurement, and why is it the best bowl to use?

Station 2 – Math Mystery – Fractions and Critical Thinking

Method of Research: Using a book and manipulatives to solve a math mystery

Highest Bloom's Taxonomy Level: Analyzing

Directions:
- With your group, read "The CD Collection Crisis" in the book *40 Fabulous Math Mysteries Kids Can't Resist.* Use the table of contents to find it.
- There are two levels available to solve this case. The levels are Challenge and Medium. If math is fairly easy for you, challenge yourself and choose Challenge!

CHALLENGE Level: Read the case and try to solve the crime, based on the clues you find while reading the case.

MEDIUM Level: Open the folder marked "MEDIUM Level" to find guided questions to help you figure out what math to use to solve the case. By answering these questions, you should be able to solve the case!

Feel free to use the CDs on the table to help you map it out!

Directions: Answer these questions when you have solved the case.
1. How many CDs did Hoover get?
2. How many CDs did Amy get?
3. How many CD's did Amos get?

Station 3 – Improper to Mixed Fractions and Fractions to Decimals and Back

Method of Research: Searching a video and listening to music for information and using books for practice

Highest Bloom's Taxonomy Level: Applying

Part I Directions: With your group, watch Mr. Duey's "Fractions" video and use it to answer the questions below.

Information to Research:

1. What do you have to do if a fraction is improper?

2. What is an improper fraction?

3. Question: How do you get rid of an improper fraction? Answer: "Take the top number _____ it by the _____ _____."

4. Question: How do you form a decimal from a fraction? Answer: "Take the top number _____ it by the _____ _____."

Information to Research:

1. Title of the Book:
   - Dewey Decimal Number -
   - Dewey "Fraction" Number -
2. Title of the Book:
   - Dewey Decimal Number -
   - Dewey "Fraction" Number -
3. Title of the Book:
   - Dewey Decimal Number -
   - Dewey "Fraction" Number -
4. Title of the Book:
   - Dewey Decimal Number -
   - Dewey "Fraction" Number -

Stations 4 and 5 – Adding Fractions with Unlike Denominators

Method of Research: Searching a subscription database for information and using books for practice

Highest Bloom's Taxonomy Level: Applying

Information to Research:

1. What is the modern formula for adding fractions?

   _____ + _____ = _____

2. **THINKING QUESTION:** Try this fraction addition problem by plugging the following numbers into the formula from above: a = 2, b = 3, c = 1, d = 4.

_____ + _____ = _____

Part II Directions: Fraction Roll Game
- With your group, read and use the Fraction Roll Instructions on the table
- Play the game!

Information to Research:

1. Who was the winner in your group?! _____

Station 6 – Simplifying

Method of Research: Searching a video for information and a book and a game for practice

Highest Bloom's Taxonomy Level: Evaluating

Part I Directions:
- Independently or with your group, go to TeacherTube - http://www.teachertube.com
- Search for and select "Simplify That Thang Math Fractions Rap"
- Watch the video and answer the questions below

Information to Research:

1. What are the students talking about simplifying?

2. What do these kids tell you to do if you have fraction trouble?

3. According to the girl, if you "simplify that thang," what grade will you get on your test?

4. **THINKING QUESTION:** Why is TeacherTube a good resource to use?

Part II Directions:
- With your group go to pages 22 & 23 in the book *Fabulous Fractions* by Lynette Long to find "Reduce It!"
- The quickest and most accurate reader in your group should read the rules to everyone in the group.
- Split into two-person teams. Each team plays with one deck of cards.
- Play the Reduce It game!!

Information to Research:

1. Who in your game ended up with the most cards? _____

2. **THINKING QUESTION:** This game should be called "Simplify It!" instead of "Reduce It!" Why?

Materials Needed for Fractions Learning Stations

Station 1 – Adding Mixed Numeral Fractions and Unlike Denominators – Subscription Database

- Gale Health Reference Center Academic database: "Having our cake and eating it with you" OR http://tinyurl.com/havingourcake
- Cooking Measurement Equivalent chart (see page 158)
- Three size mixing bowls
- Calculators

Station 2 – Math Mystery – Fractions and Critical Thinking – Book and Manipulatives

- Book: *40 Fabulous Math Mysteries Kids Can't Resist* by Martin Lee & Marcia Miller
- Folder with MEDIUM level steps (see pages 158–159)
- 17 CD cases

Station 3 – Improper to Mixed Fractions, Fractions to Decimals, and Back – Video and Books

- CD: Mr. Duey's *Class Dis-Missed* with Fractions video OR Fractions video via YouTube: http://tinyurl.com/mrdueyfractions (original: https://www.youtube.com/watch?v=V96_PjlrVQc&feature=kp)
- 20 to 25 high-interest nonfiction library books with call numbers located on the spine
- Calculators

Stations 4 and 5 (two sets of these, stay put for two rotations) – Adding Fractions with Unlike Denominators – Subscription Database, Book, and Fraction Dice

- Britannica Online School Edition database: "Arithmetic of Fractions" (Scroll down to get to it) OR http://tinyurl.com/arithoffractions (original: http://www.britannica.com/EBchecked/topic/1238455/East-Asian-mathematics/253498/The-great-early-period-1st-7th-centuries) - Scroll down to "Arithmetic of Fractions"
- Book: *Fabulous Fractions* by Lynette Long: "Fraction Roll"
- Jumbo dice with fractions on them (I use labels with fractions hand written on them to cover existing numbers)
- Scratch paper
- Pencils

Station 6 – Simplifying – Video, Book, and Game

- Website: TeacherTube: http://www.teachertube.com – Video: "Simplify That Thang Fractions Rap"

- Headphones

- Headphones sign

- Book: *Fabulous Fractions* by Lynette Long: "Reduce It!"

- 2–3 decks of cards without the royals (no Jacks, Queens, or Kings)

Rotation Song Suggestion: "Fractions" by Mr. Duey on *Class Dis-missed* CD

Station 1: Cooking Measurement Equivalents	
# of Teaspoons equal to # of Cups	
1 tsp*	1/48 cup
2tsp	1/24 cup
48 tsp	1 cup

# of Tablespoons equal to # of Cups	
1tbs**	1/16 cup
2tbs	1/8 cup
4tbs	1/4 cup
6tbs	3/8 cup
8tbs	1/2Scup
12tbs	3/4 cup
16tbs	1 cup

*teaspoon
**tablespoon

Station 2:

40 Fabulous Math Mysteries Kids Can't Resist
by Martin Lee & Marcia Miller

Case: "The CD Collection Crisis"
Medium Level

What you need to know first:

1. Emma and Lump are kid detectives with an office where their clients go to meet them.

2. The clients in this case are Hoover, Amy, & Amos

(Continued)

Reminders:

Hoover gets ½ of the 17 CD's
Amy gets 1/3 of the 17 CD's
Amos gets 1/9 of the 17 CD's

Directions: Use these guiding questions to help you solve the case.

1. Is it possible to take ½ of 17?

2. Is it possible to take 1/3 of 17

3. Is it possible to take 1/9 of 17?

4. Do ½, 1/3 and 1/9 have a common denominator that is **CLOSE** to 17?

5. Convert the original fractions to one with the lowest common denominator for 2, 3, & 9.

$$\frac{1}{2} = \underline{\quad} \qquad \frac{1}{3} = \underline{\quad} \qquad \frac{1}{9} = \underline{\quad}$$

6. Page 13, 4th paragraph. Does Hoover say he wants EXACTLY half of the collection? Is he willing to take less than half? More than half?

7. Page 13, 5th paragraph. Does Amy say she wants EXACTLY 1/3 of the collection? Is she willing to take less than 1/3? More than 1/3?

8. Page 13, 6th paragraph. Does Amos say he wants EXACTLY 1/9 of the collection? Is he willing to take less than 1/9? More than 1/9?

9. You performed the math for slightly more than 17 CDs. Based on that math, answer the three questions on Station 2.

10. If you did this correctly. The numerators you answered in question 5 will add up to 17!

Student Pre-Self-Assessment:

These questions are to be answered before the lesson takes place. The questions can be multiple choice for data collection purposes or students may fill in the blank.

1. What is a good source to use for math research? (If you haven't learned this yet or you don't know, put IDK.)

2. How do you convert a fraction to a decimal? (If you haven't learned this yet or you don't know, put IDK.)

3. What is ⅚ + ¾? (If you haven't learned this yet or you don't know, put IDK.)

4. Convert 601.233 to a fraction. (If you haven't learned this yet or you don't know, put IDK.)

Student Post-Self-Assessment:

These questions are to be answered after the lesson takes place. Any or all of the following questions can be used in an assessment of your choice (see Chapter 6) for this set of multimedia learning stations. The questions can be multiple choice for data collection purposes or students may fill in the blank.

1. What is a good source to use for math research?

2. How do you convert a fraction to a decimal?

3. What is ⅚ + ¾?

4. Convert 601.233 to a fraction.

5. What is something specific you learned today that surprised you?

6. Complete this sentence. "After today, I am still struggling with…"

7. What learning stations did you find to be the most interesting? Check all that apply.

   • Station 1 - Adding Mixed Numeral Fractions & Unlike Denominators - Subscription Databases & Recipe

   • Station 2 - Math Mystery - Book

   • Station 3 - Improper to Mixed Fractions, Fractions to Decimals, & Back - Fraction Video & Books

   • Stations 4 & 5 - Adding Fractions with Unlike Denominators - Subscription Databases, Book, & Fraction Dice

   • Station 6 - Simplifying - Video, Book, & Card Game

8. What would you change about your learning process if you were to do these stations again?

9. Overall, how would you assess your learning today?

   • I did extremely well. I learned a lot about my topic and would like to learn more. I learned some research skills to use in the future.

   • I did well. I learned something about my topic and got some tips on how to research that I can use in the future.

   • I did OK. I could have worked a little harder, but I learned something about my topic and researching.

   • I wasn't on my game today. I didn't learn nearly as much as I could have.

   • I didn't do anything today, so I didn't learn anything.

10. Kindly list any suggestions you have for improving these stations.

Big Project Assessment Option:

Student Directions:

"Think about what you learned in the library during the Fractions Multimedia Learning Stations. As a group of three or four, pick a math topic you learned about, and write your own rap song like the students did in 'Simply That Thang.'

Record a video of your version of the rap. The best one in the class will be posted on TeacherTube. Who knows?! Maybe your rap video will be used somewhere in the world for someone else's multimedia learning stations!"

Math 2

Probability, Percents, Ratios, and Proportions Learning Stations

Grade Level: 7–8

Subject Standards from Virginia Standards of Learning

Mathematics: http://www.doc.virginia.gov/testing/sol/standards_docs/mathematics/index.shtml

7th Grade: 7.4, 7.6, 7.9
8th Grade: 8.3, 8.12

AASL Standards

1 - Inquire, think critically, and gain knowledge

- 1.1 Skills – 1.1.1, 1.1.2, 1.1.6, 1.1.7, 1.1.8, 1.1.9
- 1.2 Dispositions in Action – 1.2.6, 1.2.7
- 1.3 Responsibilities – 1.3.5
- 1.4 Self-Assessment Strategies – 1.4.1, 1.4.2, 1.4.4

2 - Draw conclusions, make informed decisions, apply knowledge to new situations, and create new knowledge.

- 2.1 Skills – 2.1.1, 2.1.2, 2.1.3, 2.1.5
- 2.2 Dispositions in Action – 2.2.3, 2.2.4
- 2.3 Responsibilities – 2.3.1
- 2.4 Self-Assessment Strategies – 2.4.2, 2.4.3, 2.4.4

3 - Share knowledge and participate ethically and productively as members of our democratic society.

- 3.1 Skills – 3.1.5, 3.1.6
- 3.2 Dispositions in Action – 3.2.1, 3.2.3
- 3.3 Responsibilities – 3.3.4
- 3.4 Self-Assessment Strategies – 3.4.1, 3.4.3

Modifications for Special Education Students:

1. Have students work in teams of two or more.

2. Spread these learning stations over two ninety-minute class periods.

3. Work especially closely with students on Stations 1 and 4.

Station 1 – Ratios, Proportion, and Scale

Method of Research: Reading a website for information and tinker toys to create

Highest Bloom's Taxonomy Level: Creating

Be an Architect!

Directions: Look on the atlas provided to find a map of the United States.

Information to Research:

1. Is this map of the United States actual size?

2. In this map, was the United States cut into fraction pieces to make it small enough to fit on the page?

Hopefully, you answered No to the last two questions. The map isn't actual size, nor is it a smaller piece of the United States. In fact, it is an almost perfect "shrunken-down" version. We say this "shrunken-down" version is drawn to scale.

Directions: You will be using scale to create a "shrunken-down" version of the Willis Tower (formerly called the Sears Tower). Select the link to find the dimensions of the actual-size skyscraper. http://tinyurl.com/towerdim.

Information to Research:

1. Height (H) – _____ (*Hint: Find the height of the skyscraper without the antenna.)

2. Length (L) – _____

3. Width (W) – _____

Directions:

- Use a 1 inch to 25 feet ratio for your scale. This means every inch on your model equals 25 feet on the actual skyscraper. This can be written as a ratio 1:25 or 1/25
  - 1 = scaled inches
  - 25 = scaled feet
- Using this scale, create a proportion to determine the height, length, and width that your Tinker Toy tower needs to be.
  - Height of model = scaled inches
  - Height of skyscraper = scaled feet
- Using this proportion, cross-multiply to determine the dimensions your model skyscraper will be.

Information to Research:

Height - $\dfrac{\text{Height of model}}{\text{Height of skyscraper}} \longrightarrow \dfrac{x}{} = \dfrac{1}{25}$ (scaled inches) (scaled feet) $x = \underline{\hspace{1cm}}$

Length - $\dfrac{\text{Length of model}}{\text{Length of skyscraper}} \longrightarrow \dfrac{x}{} = \dfrac{1}{25}$ (scaled inches) (scaled feet) $x = \underline{\hspace{1cm}}$

Width - $\dfrac{\text{Width of model}}{\text{Width of skyscraper}} \longrightarrow \dfrac{x}{} = \dfrac{1}{25}$ (scaled inches) (scaled feet) $x = \underline{\hspace{1cm}}$

Directions:

- Fill in the H, L, and W on the diagram below.
- Use these dimensions to build a scaled skyscraper with the tinker toys provided. Stick to your scale measurements as much as possible.

Information to Research:

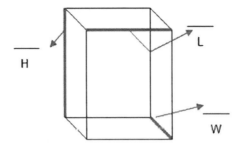

Station 2 – Probability, Ratios, Fractions, and Percents

Method of Research: Searching and reading an almanac for information

Highest Bloom's Taxonomy Level: Analyzing

Be a Political Analyst!

Directions:
- Using the almanac, search in the general index for the state you live in.
- Under your state, find "Presidential Elections."
- Look at the page numbers provided until you find the section that shows, by year, if your state voted for a democrat or a republican in the last presidential election.
- Use that information to answer the questions and complete the tasks below.

Information to Research:

1. Count how many times the people in your state voted for a democrat for president and how many times they voted for a republican for president. Look for the D or R to signify whether the person was a Democrat or a Republican. Place your answers below.

   - Democrat -

   - Republican -

2. **Odds** are often written as a ratio. We will be using the information you gathered from the almanac to calculate odds. Our odds will be democrat votes vs. republican votes. A colon (:) is used to separate the two groups.

   - What are the odds that your state will vote for a democrat for president instead of a republican in the next election? _____:_____

   - What are the odds that your state will vote for a republican for president instead of a democrat in the next election? _____:_____

3. Finding a percent chance that something will happen is different than calculating odds. When finding a percent, one group is compared to the total number of the two groups combined. One group is not compared to another group. Use the following formula to answer the next two questions.

   - In the next presidential election, what is the percent chance that your state will vote for a democrat for president?

   - In the next presidential election, what is the percent chance that your state will vote for a republican for president?

$$\frac{x\%}{100} = \underline{\hspace{2cm}} \longleftarrow \text{\# for democrat}$$
$$\longleftarrow \text{(all democrat + republican)}$$
$$x = \underline{\hspace{1.5cm}}\%$$

(Remember to **cross multiply!**)

$$\frac{x\%}{100} = \underline{\hspace{2cm}} \longleftarrow \text{\# for republican}$$
$$\longleftarrow \text{(all democrat + republican)}$$
$$x = \underline{\hspace{1.5cm}}\%$$

(Remember to **cross multiply!**)

- Add the percentages that were the answers from a. and b. (above) ____ + ____ = ____
- Is the answer 100? _____ If not, go back and redo a. and b.

Station 3 – Math Mystery Using Probability, Ratio, Proportion, and Percent

Method of Research: Using books to apply math skills

Highest Bloom's Taxonomy Level: Analyzing

Be a Game Show Contestant!

Part I Directions:
- Use the table of contents to find "Under Particular Conditions" in the book *40 Fabulous Math Mysteries Kids Can't Resist* by Martin Lee and Marcia Miller.
- Choose a quick and accurate reader from your group to read the math mystery "Under Particular Conditions" to the group.

Information to Research:

1. What is the essential question being asked?

2. How many books were on the shelf? Is this important to know in order to solve the essential question?

3. How many fantasy books were on the shelf? Is this important to know in order to solve the essential question?

4. How many of the fantasy books have a $1,000 bill in them? Is this important to solve the essential question?

   - How many –

   - Important –

5. What is the ratio of books with the dollar sign ($) in them to fantasy books? _____ : _____ Reduce the ratio. _____ : _____

6. What is the probability a fantasy book with a $1,000 bill in it will be chosen? Write the answer in ratio form. (Hint: Same answer as the last question.) _____: _____

7. What is the probability Victor will choose a book with money in it? Write your answer as a percent. To find the answer, use the ratio from above to write a proportion and calculate the percent.

$$\frac{x}{100} = \frac{\rule{1cm}{0.4pt}}{\rule{1cm}{0.4pt}}$$ ←—— (# of books with $)
←—— (# of fantasy books)

x = _____ %

Part II Directions:

• Use the Tips for Fiction and Nonfiction Books* provided below
• Use these books and the answers and formulas from Part I to help answer the questions below.

Information to Research:

1. What is the ratio of nonfiction books to total books on the cart?

2. What is the probability a student would randomly select a nonfiction book from the cart? Write your answer as a percent.

*Tips for Fiction and Nonfiction Books

• Fiction books have the first three letters of the author's last name as the call number.

- Nonfiction books have a Dewey Decimal number and the first three letters of the author's last name as the call number.

Station 4 – Probability and Ratios

Method of Research: Searching and reading databases for information

Highest Bloom's Taxonomy Level: Applying

Be a Great Game Player!

Part I Directions:
- Using the school subscription databases, search for *Probability*
- Use the information found in the database articles to answer the questions below.

Information to Research:

1. What new branch of math was created to help measure chance?

2. How is probability expressed?

3. When flipping a coin, two outcomes are possible—heads or tails. What are three (3) ways the probability of landing on heads can be expressed?

4. **THINKING QUESTION:** Does a probability ratio express certainty (something will *always* happen a definite number of times) or likeliness (something is *likely* to happen a certain number of times)?

5. When two dice are rolled, how many possible outcomes are there? _____

6. CITE YOUR SOURCE. The citation may already be provided in the database article. If not, use www.easybib.com to create one.

Information to Research:

1. Which player won the game?

2. After the game is over, discuss what was in Player #1's folder.

3. According to this probability strategy, which player should have won the game? Why?

4. How would you play this game differently, if you were to play again?

Station 5 – Probability

Method of Research: Watching and listening to a video for information

Highest Bloom's Taxonomy Level: Applying

Be a Sports Analyst!

Basketball Free Throw Video

Information to Research:

1. What is one way to determine the probability of a certain player making a free throw?

2. What is the formula for Experimental Probability?

3. If a player has made 125 free throws out of 150 attempts in a season, what percent chance does he have of making the next shot? _____

4. If the same player continues making 75% of his free throws, will his probability to make a free throw go up or down?

5. **THINKING QUESTION (Do after the video):** If a basketball player on your school's team has made 30 free throws out of 50 attempts, what is the probability he/she will make the next free throw?

OR

Baseball Batting Averages Video

Information to Research:

1. What does a baseball player's batting average measure?

2. What is the formula for calculating baseball batting average?

3. If a player has made 8 hits out of 30 attempts at bat, what is his batting average and what is the percent chance he will make a hit the next time he is at bat?

   • Batting Average –

   • Percent –

4. If the same player continues making 50% of his attempted hits, will his probability to make a hit go up or down?

5. **THINKING QUESTION (Do after the video):** If a baseball player on your school's team has made 5 hits out of 25 attempts at bat, what is the probability he will make a hit the next time he is at bat?

Materials Needed for Probability, Percents, Ratios, and Proportions Learning Stations

Station 1 – Ratios, Proportion and Scale – Website and Tinker Toys

• Tinker Toys
• Tape measure
• Ruler
• Calculators
• Atlas
• Website: http://tinyurl.com/towerdim (original: http://www.glasssteelandstone.com/BuildingDetail/375.php)

Station 2 – Probability, Ratios, Fractions, and Percents – Almanac

• Current World Almanac
• Calculators

Station 3 – Math Mystery Using Probability, Ratio, Proportion, and Percent – Books

• Book: *40 Fabulous Math Mysteries Kids Can't Resist*
• Calculators
• Cart of 35 library books: 15 fiction and 20 nonfiction

Station 4 – Probability and Ratios – School Subscription Databases and Games

• School subscription databases
• Number Chance folders (see info pages 178–180)

- 2 dice
- Copies of Number Chance score cards (see info below)

Station 5 – Probability – Discovery Education Videos

- 2 Discovery Education videos "Example 1: Historical Probability-Basketball Free" and "Example 3: Probability Batting Average"
- Calculators
- Headphones
- Headphones sign

Number Chance Info for All Players:

Number Chance Rules
All Players

Materials: Pair of dice; Number Chance Score Card; pencil

Object: To get the most points at the end of three rounds of the game

Set Up: Choose a score keeper (the score keeper rolls the dice, counts and adds the score, but doesn't play); players stand around the table; put all players name on the score sheet;

Play:
The score keeper rolls a pair of dice. Whatever the total number on the dice is, is added on the score sheet under Round 1 for each player. For example, if the score keeper rolls a 7, then every player gets a 7 under Round 1 (see below).

	Round 1	Round 2	Round 3	Total
Player #1	7			
Player #2	7			
Player #3	7			
Player #4	7			
Player #5	7			
Player #6	7			

If a player wants to keep that score, he/she sits down and the score is circled on the score sheet.

Each player still standing rolls the dice again.

If the **total sum** of the dice is 2, 3 or 12, all players still standing score a 0 for Round 1 and sit down.

Under the Round 1 box, if the total is any other number, this score gets added to the original score already **in the Round 1 box**.

Number Chance Score Card

	Round 1	Round 2	Round 3	Total
Player Example	7 + 8 + 11 = 26	2 + 9 + 7 + 9 = 27	2 + 7 + 8 + 6 + 5 = 28	81
Player #1				
Player #2				
Player #3				
Player #4				
Player #5				
Player #6				

Any player who wants keeps his/her score, sits down, adds the total score for Round 1 and circles it on the score sheet.

Once every player is seated, the round is over.

Continue following all the steps above for Rounds 2 & 3.

Play three rounds of the game and add three game scores for each player. The player with the highest *total score* wins.

Work Cited

Smith, Sanderson M. "Sophisticated Probability with Simple Dice Game." Herkimer's Hideaway. 2009. Web. 19 Feb 2010. <http://www.herkimershideaway.org/writings/cmlink.htm>.

Number Chance Info for Player #1

I'm going to give you a probability tip that is *only for you*. Don't share this tip with the other players!

You can use probability to determine the *likelihood* of when a 2, 3 or 12 will be rolled. You can use this information to decide when to sit down in the game and keep your score.

You learned in Part I of this station (in the database) that if two dice are rolled there are 36 possible combinations.

In this game you do not want to roll a 2, 3 or 12:

- There is only one way to roll a 2 (1 & 1)
- There are two ways to roll a 3 (1 & 2 or 2 & 1)
- There is one way to roll a 12 (6 & 6)

So, it is possible to roll a 2, 3 or 12 *four* different ways. That means we are *likely* to roll a 2, 3, or 12 *four* out of 36 times.

As a ratio it can be written as 4:36, 4 to 36 or 4/36. If we reduce that we get 1/9. So... you are likely to roll a 2, 3, or 12 *once in every nine* rolls. I would recommend you **sit down after eight rolls** of the dice (before the ninth roll).

This is your task. Remain standing until the dice have been rolled eight times. Then sit down.

* Remember probability deals with chance and *likeliness*, so although this hint doesn't guarantee you will win, it certainly will increase your probability to win!

Number Chance Score Card

	Round 1	Round 2	Round 3	Total
Player Example	7 + 8 + 11 = 26	2 + 9 + 7 + 9 = 27	2 + 7 + 8 + 6 + 5 = 28	81
Player #1				
Player #2				
Player #3				
Player #4				
Player #5				
Player #6				

Student Pre-Self-Assessment:

These questions are to be answered before the lesson takes place. The questions can be multiple choice for data collection purposes or students may fill in the blank.

1. What is a good source to use for math research? (If you haven't learned this yet or you don't know, put IDK.)

2. When can scale be used? (If you haven't learned this yet or you don't know, put IDK.)

3. Give an example of probability being used in sports. (If you haven't learned this yet or you don't know, put IDK.)

4. What kind of career can you have that uses math other than being a math teacher or librarian? (If you haven't learned this yet or you don't know, put IDK.)

Student Post-Self-Assessment:

These questions are to be answered after the lesson takes place. Any or all of the following questions can be used in an assessment of your choice (see Chapter 6) for this set of multimedia learning stations. The questions can be multiple choice for data collection purposes or students may fill in the blank.

1. What is a good source to use for research?

2. When can scale be used?

3. Give an example of probability being used in sports.

4. What kind of career can you have that uses math, other than being a math teacher or librarian?

5. What is something specific you learned today that surprised you?

6. Complete this sentence: "After today, I am still struggling with . . ."

7. What learning stations did you find to be the most interesting? Check all that apply.

   • Station 1 - Ratios, Proportion and Scale - Website and Tinker Toys

   • Station 2 - Probability, Ratios, Fractions, and Percents - Almanac

   • Station 3 - Math Mystery Using Probability, Ratio, Proportion, and Percent - Books

   • Station 4 - Probability and Ratios - Subscription Databases and Game

   • Station 5 - Probability - Discovery Education Videos

8. What would you change about your learning process if you were to do these stations again?

9. Overall, how would you assess your learning today?

   - I did extremely well. I learned a lot about my topic and would like to learn about more. I learned some research skills I can use in the future.

   - I did well. I learned something about my topic and some tips on how to research that I can use in the future.

   - I did OK. I could have worked a little harder, but I learned something about my topic and researching.

   - I wasn't on my game today. I didn't learn nearly as much as I could have.

   - I didn't do anything today, so I didn't learn anything.

10. Kindly list any suggestions you have for improving these stations.

Big Project Assessment Option:

Student Directions:

Expanding on the processes you learned and used during the library multimedia stations, research how often Target marks down its sale merchandise, and at what increments they markdown their items. Use the following blog post to help you determine this: http://thekrazycouponlady.com/style/code-red-how-to-read-target-clearance-tags/.

Research Questions:

When Target marks down an item, at what percent off do they typically begin?
How often do they mark down sale items even further, after the initial markdown?
After the initial sale price, what other cycles of "percents off" do they go through?

Student Directions:

Find an item you would like to buy at Target (http://www.target.com/). The item you choose should be more than $20. Use it to create an infographic of an item's lifetime at Target.

You may use an infographic-generating website to create the infographic for the sales cycle of the item you chose. There should be five stops of discounts after the initial list price.

At each discount stop along the way of creating your infographic, include what the new price of the item would be. The last stop on the infographic, after five rounds of discounts, can be your house.

You may use one of the following websites to create your infographic:

- Easel.ly - http://www.easel.ly/

- Pictochart - http://piktochart.com/

Math 3

Slope Learning Stations

Grade Level: 7–9 Algebra

Subject Standards from Virginia Standards of Learning

Mathematics: http://www.doe.virginia.gov/testing/sol/standards_docs/mathematics/index.shtml

Algebra: A.6

AASL Standards

1 - Inquire, think critically, and gain knowledge

- 1.1 Skills – 1.1.1, 1.1.2, 1.1.6, 1.1.7, 1.1.8, 1.1.9
- 1.2 Dispositions in Action – 1.2.1, 1.2.6
- 1.3 Responsibilities – 1.3.4, 1.3.5
- 1.4 Self-Assessment Strategies – 1.4.2, 1.4.4

2 - Draw conclusions, make informed decisions, apply knowledge to new situations, and create new knowledge

- 2.1 Skills – 2.1.1, 2.1.2, 2.1.3, 2.1.4, 2.1.5, 2.1.6
- 2.2 Dispositions in Action – 2.2.2, 2.2.3, 2.2.4
- 2.3 Responsibilities – 2.3.1, 2.3.3
- 2.4 Self-Assessment Strategies – 2.4.1, 2.4.2, 2.4.3, 2.4.4

3 - Share knowledge and participate ethically and productively as members of our democratic society

- 3.2 Dispositions in Action – 3.2.1, 3.2.2, 3.2.3
- 3.4 Self-Assessment Strategies – 3.4.1, 3.4.3

Modifications for Special Education Students:

1. Have students work in teams of two or more.
2. Spread these learning stations over two 90-minute class periods
3. Station 2 - Work with whole group to teach them how to use Google Earth
4. Station 3 - Assign the teacher or librarian to work with students through the thought processes and math necessary to complete this station
5. Station 4 - Remove two of the equations from Part II.

Station 1 – Roller Coasters and Positive, Negative, Zero, and Undefined Slope

Method of Research: Searching a video for information and using a website to create a roller coaster to apply the information

Highest Bloom's Taxonomy Level: Creating

Information to Research:

Using the information you learned from the "Slope Dude" video, determine if the four slopes below are positive, negative, zero, or undefined. Write your answer under the line of slope.

THINKING QUESTIONS:

1. Why can't you use undefined slope in your roller coaster design?

2. Is it possible to make the slope of a hill too steep on a roller coaster? Explain your answer.

Station 2 – Ski Slopes & Determining and Graphing Slope

Method of Research: Watching a video for information and using Google Earth to analyze ski slope steepness and difficulty

Highest Bloom's Taxonomy Level: Analyzing

Information to Research:

1. What are two things slope can tell us?

2. "The higher the _____ _____ of the line, the steeper the slope will be."

3. **THINKING QUESTION:** If you were looking for a mountain on which to ski, what kind of slope would you like to have? Why?

4. What made Pam or Randy's slope the steepest slope in this video?

Part II Directions: Look up slope in the dictionary. You may use a print or online dictionary.

Slope –

Part III Directions: Use Google Earth to find the slope of a ski slope near you.
- Open Google Earth
- Search for a ski resort area (examples in or near Virginia are Wintergreen, VA; Massanutten, VA; Snowshoe, WV)
- Once Google Earth zooms in to one of these locations, look for white ski slopes and zoom in on one of the ski slopes.

Information to Research:

1. Click on one end of a ski slope. Look at the bottom of the Google Earth window for elevation. What is the elevation?

2. Click on the other end of the same ski slope. Look at the bottom of the Google Earth window for elevation. What is the elevation?

3. Subtract the smaller elevation from the larger elevation. _____ - _____ = _____ (The answer is the rise of the slope.)

4. What is the elevation (rise) of the ski slope you chose (see answer from #3)?

   Select the ruler tool at the top of Google Earth. Click onto the top of the ski slope, then again at the bottom of the ski slope which will draw a line. Look in the ruler box at Length. Change it to feet. This is the distance (run). What is the distance (run)?

5. Determine the slope of the ski slope using rise over run. Rise/Run = Slope

6. Compare the slope of your ski slope to that of the other members in your group. Who had the steepest slope?

7. How is slope connected to the difficulty of a ski slope?

Station 3 – Grade, Graphing Slope, Building Roads

Method of Research: Search an online road manual to determine safety of a proposed road

Highest Bloom's Taxonomy Level: Evaluating

Grade of a road is rise over run times 100. Grade = rise/run *100

> **Part I Directions:** Use a Forestry Road Best Management Practices Manual to test the practicality of a model road.
> - Control-click on http://tinyurl.com/roadslope to bring up a best practice manual for building forest roads.
> - Once on the website, use the Find feature to search for "log truck"

Information to Research:

What is the maximum grade [slope in percent] of a log truck road? _____

> **Part II Directions:** Measure the rise and run of the model road.

Information to Research:

1. Using a yard stick or measuring tape, measure the height (rise) in inches of the road track. What is the height (rise)?

2. Using a ruler or measuring tape, measure the length (run) in inches of the road track. What is the length (run)?

3. Use rise over run to determine the slope. What is the slope of the model road?

4. Multiply the slope (answer from the previous question) by 100 to get the grade (slope in percent). What is the grade? _____ %

5. Is this slope too steep for a log truck road? Would this track be suitable for log trucks? Why?

6. **THINKING QUESTION:** If you were the supervisor of this road design project, what choice would you make about the road? Defend your answer.

7. **THINKING QUESTION:** What do you think would happen if a truck full of logs were to try to ascend this slope?

8. Would the slope of the road need to be:

    a. Lowered

    b. Raised

    c. Kept the same

    d. It's not possible to determine

9. Use the information in the manual about the maximum grade a road can be, and assume the run of our model needs to stay the same. What is the tallest height (rise) our model should be to meet the standards set forth by the road manual? Think through reversing the math with your group to determine the answer.

Station 4 – Lines, Parameters, and Slope-Intercept Form

Method of Research: Search through and read a subscription database for information

Highest Bloom's Taxonomy Level: Applying

> **Part I Directions:** Use the school subscription databases to search for "line."

Information to Research:

1. What is a line?

2. What did Euclid claim about a line?

3. How can a line be represented on a coordinate plane?

4. What is the formula for slope-intercept form?

5. In the equation for slope-intercept form, what do the m and b variables represent?

   - m –

   - b –

6. Cite this source - (it is often found in the database article)

Part II Directions: Determine ordered pairs from slope-intercept form equation. and graph it.
- Use the whiteboard displaying the formula for slope intercept form. Replace the variables in the formula with the number values that have been provided. (Ex. replace *m* with *2* and *b* with *4*.)
- Using the formula, calculate three sets of ordered pairs for each equation and fill in the values for y in the tables provided. (Ex. $y = 2(0) + 4$, so $y = 4$ - the first ordered pair is (0,4).)
- On the large graphs provided, use Play-Doh to plot your points and use the string to make the line in order to graph the equation.
- Also fill in your answers on the graphs below (if you have time).

Information to Research:

REMEMBER: $y = mx + b$

Equations to solve and graph (only graph here if you have time left):

1. m = 2; b = 4

x	y
0	
-1	
-2	

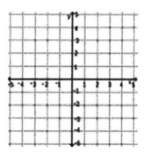

2. m = -2; b = -3

x	y
0	
1	
-1	

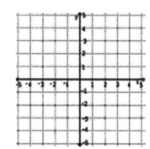

(Continued)

3. m = -1 ; b = 4

x	y
0	
1	
2	

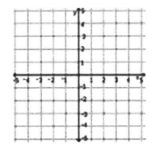

4. m = 2 ; b = -4

x	y
0	
1	
2	

Materials Needed for Slope Learning Stations

*Two sets of the same stations are needed, so double all materials

Station 1 – Roller Coasters and Positive, Negative, Zero, and Undefined Slope – Video, Website, Model Roller Coaster

- TeacherTube Video – "Slope Dude"
- K'NEX Star Shooter Roller Coaster kit (put together)
- Four Labels: *Positive*, *Negative*, *Zero*, and *Undefined*
- Roller coaster design website: http://tinyurl.com/rollercoasterdesign (original: http://tv.disney.go.com/disney channel/phineasandferb/games/rollercoaster/)
- Headphones
- Headphones sign

Station 2 – Ski Slopes and Determining and Graphing Slope – Video and Google Earth

- Discovery Education Video – "Steepness" [3:55]
- Dictionary (print or online)
- Google Earth
- Headphones
- Headphones sign

Station 3 – Grade, Graphing Slope, Building Roads – Website, Road Manual, K'NEX Truck Road

- Finger Lakes Forest: Best Management Practices During a Timber Harvest: Online Road Manual website: http://tinyurl.com/roadslope (original http://www2.dnr.cornell.edu/ext/bmp/contents/during/dur_roads.htm)

- Yard stick or measuring tape

- K'NEX Monster Jam Grave Digger Downhill Thrill set (put together)

Station 4 – Lines, Parameters, and Slope-Intercept Form – Subscription Databases, Graphs, and Play-Doh

- School subscription databases – "line"

- White board

- Easel for the white board

- 36-inch^2 graph (can be made with poster paper)

- Four colors of Play-Doh

- String

- Numbers and variables with magnets stuck on the back

Student Pre-Self-Assessment:

These questions are to be answered before the lesson takes place. The questions can be multiple choice for data collection purposes or students may fill in the blank.

1. What is a good source to use for math research? (If you haven't learned this yet or you don't know, put IDK.)

2. How can you determine the steepness of a ski slope? (If you haven't learned this yet or you don't know, put IDK.)

3. Why is the grade of a log road important? (If you haven't learned this yet or you don't know, put IDK.)

4. What is the formula for slope-intercept form? (If you haven't learned this yet or you don't know, put IDK.)

Student Post-Self-Assessment:

These questions are to be answered after the lesson takes place. Any or all of the following questions can be used in an assessment of your choice (see Chapter 6) for this set of multimedia learning stations. The questions can be multiple choice for data collection purposes or students may fill in the blank.

1. What is a good source to use for math research?

2. How can you determine the steepness of a ski slope?

3. Why is the grade of a log road important?

4. What is the formula for slope-intercept form?

5. What is something specific you learned today that surprised you?

6. Complete this sentence. "After today, I am still struggling with…"

7. What learning stations did you find to be the most interesting? Check all that apply.
   - Station 1 - Roller Coasters and Positive, Negative, Zero, and Undefined Slope - Video, Website, Model Roller Coaster
   - Station 2 - Ski Slopes, and Determining and Graphing Slope - Video and Google Earth
   - Station 3 - Grade, Graphing Slope, Building Roads - Website, Road Manual, K'NEX Truck Road
   - Station 4 - Lines, Parameters, and Slope-Intercept Form - Subscription Databases, Graphs, and Play-Doh

8. What would you change about your learning process if you were to do these stations again?

9. Overall, how would you assess your learning today?
   - I did extremely well. I learned a lot about my topic and would like to learn more. I learned some research skills to use in the future.
   - I did well. I learned something about my topic and learned some tips on how to research that I can use in the future.
   - I did OK. I could have worked a little harder, but I learned something about my topic and researching.
   - I wasn't on my game today. I didn't learn nearly as much as I could have.
   - I didn't do anything today, so I didn't learn anything.

10. Kindly list any suggestions you have for improving these stations:

Big Project Assessment Option:

Have students create a video where they, or a character they create, teach others how work through a mathematical slope problem. Require students to either be the character themselves or to create an animated character for this video. They may not film another person doing the slope problem. Also, require that diagrams and visuals be included in the video with an explanation for the method of solving the problem.

If students choose to create animated videos, some Web 2.0 tools available to do this are GoAnimate (http://goanimate.com/), PowToon (http://www.powtoon.com/), or Moovly (http://www.moovly.com/).

Math 4

Surface Area and Volume Learning Stations

Grade Level: 7–8

Subject Standards from Virginia Standards of Learning

Mathematics: http://www.doe.virginia.gov/testing/sol/standards_docs/mathematics/index.shtml

7th Grade: 7.5
8th Grade: 8.7

AASL Standards

1. Inquire, think critically, and gain knowledge

   - 1.1 Skills – 1.1.1, 1.1.2, 1.1.6, 1.1.7, 1.1.8, 1.1.9

   - 1.2 Dispositions in Action - 1.2.5, 1.2.6

   - 1.3 Responsibilities – 1.3.5

   - 1.4 Self-Assessment Strategies – 1.4.1, 1.4.2, 1.4.3, 1.4.4

2. Draw conclusions, make informed decisions, apply knowledge to new situations, and create new knowledge

   - 2.1 Skills – 2.1.1, 2.1.3, 2.1.5

   - 2.2 Dispositions in Action – 2.2.3

   - 2.3 Responsibilities - 2.3.1

   - 2.4 Self-Assessment Strategies - 2.4.2, 2.4.3, 2.4.4

3. Share knowledge and participate ethically and productively as members of our democratic society

   - 3.2 Dispositions in Action - 3.2.2, 3.2.3

   - 3.4 Self-Assessment Strategies - 3.4.1, 3.4.3

Modifications for Special Education Students:

1. Students often need extra help with the math in Stations 2 and 3.

2. Station 3 - Help students understand the relationship between the NETS and the 3D prism that are constructed from then.

3. Station 3 - Sometimes students have difficulty folding and attaching the NETS in order for them to become 3D

4. Station 3 - Students need extra help measuring the NETS and plugging the measurements into the formulas.

Station 1 – Real-World Surface Area and Volume

Method of Research: Watching and listening to a video for information.

Highest Bloom's Taxonomy Level: Remembering

> **Part I Directions:**
> - Login to Discovery Education (www.discoveryeducation.com) and complete a search for "Area Cylinder"
> - From the results, select and play the video "Example 2: Properties of Rectangular Prisms and Cylinders"

Information to Research:

1. What is an example from the video of a real-world rectangular prism?

2. How can you find the area of a rectangular prism?

3. What is the formula for calculating the surface area of a rectangular prism?

4. What is an example from the video of a real-world cylinder?

5. What is a cylinder?

6. When the surface of a cylinder unwraps, what shape does it make?

7. What is the formula for calculating the surface area of a cylinder?

8. **THINKING QUESTION:** Give an example of a real-world rectangular prism and a real-world cylinder that was not including in the video.

Part II Directions:
- 1. In the search box of Discovery Education, type Pool Volume
- 2. Select and play Example 2: Volume – Pools (1:50)

Information to Research:

1. What is volume and how is volume expressed?

   a. What is it –

   b. How is it expressed –

2. What are cubic units based on?

3. What is the formula for the volume of a rectangular prism?

4. How many cubic feet of water are found in the pool in the example?

5. How many cubic feet of water are found in the shark aquarium?

Station 2 – Applying Knowledge of Surface Area & Volume

Method of Research: Reading a website for information and using it to apply math skills

Highest Bloom's Taxonomy Level: Applying

Directions:
- Go to the website http://tinyurl.com/annlearner
- Use the information given to answer the questions

Information to Research:

1. When someone wraps a gift, is the wrapping paper that is covering the box surface area or volume?

2. Does milk poured in a glass fill the surface area or the volume of the glass?

---

3. What is surface area?

4. What is volume?

Information to Research:

1. How many faces (squares) are in a cube?

2. What does the net (the unfolded shape) look like for a cube?

3. If each side of a cube is 4 inches long, what would the surface area be? **Hint:** figure out the area of each square (length x width) and multiply it by six (for the six faces on the cube).

Information to Research:

What is the equation for calculating the surface area of a cylinder?

Information to Research:

1. The circumference of the circle in this diagram is_____

2. The area of the rectangle is (hint: the width is 8) _____

3. The area for each of the cylinder's circle bases is _____

4. When adding all of those areas together, you find the total surface area is _____

Information to Research:

1. How many unit cubes did it take to form the bottom layer of the cube shown?

2. How many of these layers would it take to fill the entire cube?

3. In total, how many of the unit cubes were needed to fill the polyhedron?

Directions:
- At the bottom of the page, select Volume: Cylinders.
- Scroll down, read the text under Find the Volume of a Cylinder, then select NEXT.
- Then work on the questions on the right side of the picture.
- You will need to plug your answers into the blanks on the computer (THEN HIT ENTER), and answer them on this document.

Information to Research:

1. What is the area of the circular base of the cylinder?

2. What is the height of the cylinder?

3. What is the volume of the cylinder?

Station 3 – Visualizing Surface Area and Volume

Method of Research: Using a website to manipulate shapes and building nets to visualize concepts

Highest Bloom's Taxonomy Level: Evaluating

Part I Directions:
- Go to the following website: http://tinyurl.com/savolume
- Scroll down and look at the rectangular prism created when the width, depth, and height are all 10.
- Use the information to answer the questions below.

Information to Research:

1. What is the volume of this shape? What is the surface area? Is the volume or the surface area bigger?

    a. Volume –

    b. Surface area –

    c. Biggest –

Directions: Change the Width of the shape to 1 by sliding the scroll bar next to it.

Information to Research:

2. What is the volume of this shape? What is the surface area? Which is bigger?

    a. Volume –

    b. Surface area –

    c. Biggest –

3. **THINKING QUESTION:** Look at the shapes when the width is 10 and when it is 1. Explain why you think the volume is bigger in the first example, but the surface area is bigger in the second example?

For the CUBE net: Formula: $6s^2$

What you need to know first:

- "s" indicates length of a side

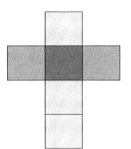

Information to Research:

1. Who in your group was in charge of the cube?

2. Define your variable (convert fractions to decimals): s = _____

3. What is the surface area of the cube in square inches?

For the CYLINDER net: Formula: $2\Pi r^2 + 2\Pi r\,h$

What you need to know first:

- Π = 3.14

- r means radius (half the diameter of the circle)

- h means height of the cylinder

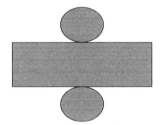

Information to Research:

1. Define your variables (convert fractions to decimals): r = _____; h = _____

2. What is the surface area of the cylinder in square inches?

Materials Needed for Surface Area and Volume Learning Stations

Station 1 – Real-World Surface Area and Volume – Discovery Education Video

- Two Discovery Education Videos: "Example 3: Surface Area – Pyramid and Cylinder" (3:00) and "Example 2: Volume – Pools" (1:50)

- Headphones
- Headphones sign

Station 2 – Applying Knowledge of Surface Area and Volume – Website

- Annenberg Learner Interactives website: http://tinyurl.com/annlearner (original: http://www.learner.org/interactives/geometry/area.html)

Station 3 – Visualizing Surface Area and Volume – Website and Nets

- Inter*activate* Surface Area and Volume Website: http://tinyurl.com/savolume (original: http://www.shodor.org/interactivate/activities/SurfaceAreaAndVolume/)
- Nets for a cube and a cylinder photocopied on different colored paper (pre-cut)
- 3D models of the two nets (two sets, if having two sets of stations)
- Rulers
- Glue sticks or scotch tape
- Calculators (hand-held or online)

Student Pre-Self-Assessment:

These questions are to be answered before the lesson takes place. The questions can be multiple choice for data collection purposes or students may fill in the blank.

1. What is a good source to use for math research? (If you haven't learned this yet or you don't know, put IDK.)
2. What is a real-world example of a rectangular prism, and what is a real-world example of a cylinder? (If you haven't learned this yet or you don't know, put IDK.)

NET for Cube

NET for Cylinder

3. What is surface area? (If you haven't learned this yet or you don't know, put IDK.)

4. What is volume? (If you haven't learned this yet or you don't know, put IDK.)

5. What is a net? (If you haven't learned this yet or you don't know, put IDK.)

Student Post-Self-Assessment:

These questions are to be answered after the lesson takes place. Any or all of the following questions can be used in an assessment of your choice (see Chapter 6) for this set of multimedia learning stations. The questions can be multiple choice for data collection purposes or students may fill in the blank.

1. What is a good source to use for research?

2. What is a real-world example of a rectangular prism, and what is a real-world example of a cylinder?

3. What is surface area?

4. What is volume?

5. What is a net?

6. Complete this sentence. "After today, I am still struggling with . . ."

7. What learning stations did you find to be the most interesting? Check all that apply.

   • Station 1 - Real-World Surface Area and Volume - Discovery Education Video

   • Station 2 - Applying Knowledge of Surface Area & Volume - Website

   • Station 3 - Visualizing Surface Area and Volume - Website & Nets

8. What would you change about your learning process if you were to do these stations again?

9. Overall, how would you assess your learning today?

   • I did extremely well. I learned a lot about my topic and would like to learn more. I learned some research skills to use in the future.

   • I did well. I learned something about my topic and some tips on how to research that I can use in the future.

   • I did OK. I could have worked a little harder, but I learned something about my topic and researching.

- I wasn't on my game today. I didn't learn nearly as much as I could have.

- I didn't do anything today, so I didn't learn anything.

10. Kindly list any suggestions you have for improving these stations:

Big Project Assessment Option:

Have students use SketchUp (http://www.sketchup.com/) (formerly Google SketchUp) to design a pool for their backyard. They need to include measurements and dimensions of the pool, and to calculate the surface area and volume of the pool.

They should then justify the overall size of the pool they designed, explaining why it is a good fit for their lives, and for the size of their backyard. They should justify why this size pool is not too big and not too small, but why it is just right.

Essential Questions:

What dimensions for a pool be for your backyard? How long, how wide and how deep should it be?

What is the surface area of the pool?

How many gallons of water would this take?

Why is this the perfect size pool for you and your family?

Science 1

Biomes Learning Stations

Grade Level: 6–7 (Life Science)

Subject Standards from Virginia Standards of Learning

Science: http://www.doe.virginia.gov/testing/sol/standards_docs/science/index.shtml

Life Science: LS.9

AASL Standards

1. Inquire, think critically, and gain knowledge
   - 1.1 Skills – 1.1.2, 1.1.6, 1.1.7, 1.1.8, 1.1.9
   - 1.2 Dispositions in Action – 1.2.2, 1.2.3, 1.2.6, 1.2.7
   - 1.3 Responsibilities – 1.3.5
   - 1.4 Self-Assessment Strategies – 1.4.1, 1.4.3, 1.4.4

2. Draw conclusions, make informed decisions, apply knowledge to new situations, and create new knowledge
   - 2.1 Skills – 2.1.2, 2.1.3, 2.1.4, 2.1.5
   - 2.2 Dispositions in Action – 2.2.1, 2.2.4
   - 2.4 Self-Assessment Strategies – 2.4.2, 2.4.3, 2.4.4

3. Share knowledge and participate ethically and productively as members of our democratic society
   - 3.2 Dispositions in Action – 3.2.3
   - 3.4 Self-Assessment Strategies – 3.4.1, 3.4.3

Modifications for Special Education Students:

1. Have students work with a partner.

2. Spread this research over two ninety-minute class periods instead of one.

Station 1 – Deciduous Forest (Temperate)

Method of Research: Using a Web 2.0 Tool and reading websites for information

Highest Bloom's Taxonomy Level: Remembering

> **Directions:** As a group, use ThingLink to find more information on the Deciduous Forest (Temperate) Biome.

1. Go to http://tinyurl.com/biomethinglink.

2. Move your cursor over the picture on the website. Red circles will appear with a heading. These are the links to use to find information.

3. Search through the websites to find information on Deciduous Forests (you may find it listed under Temperate)

4. Use Control-F to get a Find box to search for keywords on a webpage

5. Fill in the chart ONLY for Station 1: Deciduous Forest (Temperate)

Station 2 – Desert

Method of Research: Reading books and eBooks for information

Highest Bloom's Taxonomy Level: Remembering

> **Directions:** Use the books and eBooks provided to discover more about the Desert Biome

1. Use the Tables of Contents and Indexes of these books to help you find specific information
2. When using eBooks, use the keyword search
3. Fill in the chart ONLY for Station 2: Desert

Station 3 – Grassland

Method of Research: Searching subscription databases for information

Highest Bloom's Taxonomy Level: Remembering

> **Directions:** Use the school subscription databases to research the Grassland Biome

1. If the first article you try doesn't give you all the information you need, choose another article
2. Fill in the chart ONLY for Station 3: Grassland

Station 4 – Tundra

Method of Research: Reading print and electronic reference books for information

Highest Bloom's Taxonomy Level: Remembering

> **Directions:** Use the reference books (print and electronic) provided to find information on the Tundra Biome.

1. You may need to use the index of the encyclopedias to find information
2. When using electronic reference books, use the keyword search to find information
3. Fill in the chart ONLY for Station 4: Tundra

Station 5 – Coniferous Forest (Taiga)

Method of Research: Effectively using Google Advanced Search to find reliable websites and reading them for information

Highest Bloom's Taxonomy Level: Applying

1. Go to Google – http://www.google.com/advanced_search

2. Type "Biome" in the blank next to "Find pages with . . . all these words"

3. Type "Coniferous Forest" in the blank next to "this exact word or phrase" (so it will search coniferous forest, not coniferous *and* forest)

4. Type "Wikipedia" in the blank next to "none of these words"

5. Type .gov in the blank next to "site or domain" (so it will only search .gov sites)

6. Select Advanced Search and choose from the search results. You may use more than one search result.

7. Fill in the chart *only* for Station 5: Coniferous Forest (Taiga)

Station 6 – Rainforest

Method of Research: Choosing reliable resources for researching and searching them for information

Highest Bloom's Taxonomy Level: Applying

Directions: Use any of the sources from Stations 1 to 5 to seek information on the Rainforest Biome.

1. Source Options: Websites found on ThingLink, books and eBooks, Google Advanced Search, reference books (print and electronic), or school subscription databases

2. **Hint:** If you use a source and it doesn't help you, try a different type of source. Sometimes in research you will hit a dead end, and you will have to redirect your search.

3. Fill in the chart for Station 6: Rainforest

	Station 1: **Deciduous Forest (Temperate)**	Station 2: **Desert**	Station 3: **Grassland**	Station 4: **Tundra**	Station 5: **Coniferous Forest (Taiga)**	Station 6: **Rainforest**
General Description						
Climate						
Animals						
Animal Adaptations						
Plants						
Plant Adaptations						
Two absolutely, completely and totally thrilling details or facts!	1. 2.	1. 2.	1. 2.	1. 2.	1. 2.	1. 2.

Biomes Learning Stations Chart

Materials Needed for Biomes Learning Stations

Station 1 – Deciduous Forest (Temperate) – Websites/ThingLink

- ThingLink of seven Websites – http://tinyurl.com/biomethinglink (original: https://www.thinglink.com/scene/564484644804755457)

    ◦ http://www.mbgnet.net/

    ◦ http://www.enchantedlearning.com/biomes/

    ◦ http://www.ucmp.berkeley.edu/glossary/gloss5/biome/

    ◦ http://www.worldbiomes.com/

    ◦ https://php.radford.edu/~swoodwar/biomes/?page_id=94

    ◦ http://www.worldbiomes.com/

    ◦ https://askabiologist.asu.edu/explore/biomes

Station 2 – Desert – Books and eBooks

- Many library books and eBooks on deserts

Station 3 – Grassland – Databases

- School subscription databases: "Grassland"

Station 4 – Tundra – Reference Books (print and electronic)

- General encyclopedia sets (print or electronic)
- Biome reference books and eBooks

Station 5 – Coniferous Forest – Advanced Google Searching

- Google Advanced Search - site or domain search limited to .gov

Station 6 – Rainforest – Free Choice of Previous Five Search Strategies

- Books and eBooks (catalog)
- Reference Books - print and electronic (catalog)
- School subscription databases
- ThingLink with websites - Same as Station 1
- Google Advanced Search - site or domain search limited to .gov

Rotation Song Suggestion: "Bare Necessities" from *The Jungle Book* Soundtrack

Student Pre-Self-Assessment:

These questions are to be answered before the lesson takes place. The questions can be multiple choice for data collection purposes or students may fill in the blank.

1. State one fact about the Grassland Biome. (If you haven't learned this yet or you don't know, put IDK.)

2. What are some animal adaptations in the Tundra Biome? (If you haven't learned this yet or you don't know, put IDK.)

3. What are some plant adaptations in the Desert Biome? (If you haven't learned this yet or you don't know, put IDK.)

4. What question do you have about the Rainforest Biome? (If you haven't learned this yet or you don't know, put IDK.)

5. What is the difference between the Deciduous Forest Biome and the Coniferous Forest Biome? (If you haven't learned this yet or you don't know, put IDK.)

6. What is a good resource to use to find research? (If you haven't learned this yet or you don't know, put IDK.)

Student Post-Self-Assessment:

These questions are to be answered after the lesson takes place. Any or all of the following questions can be used in an assessment of your choice (see Chapter 6) for this set of multimedia learning stations. The questions can be multiple choice for data collection purposes or students may fill in the blank.

1. State one fact about the Grassland Biome.

2. What are some animal adaptations in the Tundra Biome?

3. What are some plant adaptations in the Desert Biome?

4. What is something new you learned about the Rainforest Biome today?

5. What is the difference between the Deciduous Forest Biome and the Coniferous Forest Biome?

6. Which resource did you most like using today?
   - Websites/ThingLink
   - Books and eBooks
   - School subscription databases
   - Reference Books (print and electronic)
   - Google Advanced Searching

7. What learning stations did you find to be the most interesting? Check all that apply.
   - Station 1 - Deciduous Forest (Temperate) – Websites/ThingLink
   - Station 2 - Desert – Books and eBooks
   - Station 3 - Grassland – School Subscription Databases
   - Station 4 - Tundra – Reference Books (print and electronic)
   - Station 5 - Coniferous Forest – Advanced Google Searching
   - Station 6 - Rainforest – Free Choice of Previous Five Search Strategies

8. What would you change about your learning process if you were to do these stations again?

9. Overall, how would you assess your learning today?

- I did extremely well. I learned a lot about my topic and would like to learn more. I learned some research skills to use in the future.

- I did well. I learned something about my topic and some tips on how to research that I can use in the future.

- I did OK. I could have worked a little harder, but I learned something about my topic and researching.

- I wasn't on my game today. I didn't learn nearly as much as I could have.

- I didn't do anything today, so I didn't learn anything.

10. Kindly list any suggestions you have for improving these stations:

Big Project Assessment Option:

Student Directions:

Use Animoto (http://animoto.com/) to create a music video with pictures and text for one of the biomes you researched in the library during the multimedia learning stations. Many copyright-free music selections are provided for you to use.

You will need to include at least one picture and a slide of text for each section of the chart. Those include a general description, climate, animals, animal adaptations, plants, plant adaptation, and two thrilling facts of your choice.

Science 2

Cells Learning Stations

Grade Level: 7–10 (Life Science and Biology)

Subject Standards from Virginia Standards of Learning

Science: http://www.doe.virginia.gov/testing/sol/standards_docs/science/index.shtml

Life Science: LS.2, LS.3
Biology: BIO.3

AASL Standards

1. Inquire, think critically, and gain knowledge

   - 1.1 Skills – 1.1.2, 1.1.6, 1.1.7, 1.1.8, 1.1.9

   - 1.2 Dispositions in Action – 1.2.6

   - 1.3 Responsibilities – 1.3.5

2. Draw conclusions, make informed decisions, apply knowledge to new situations, and create new knowledge

   - 2.1 Skills – 2.1.3, 2.1.5

   - 2.2 Dispositions in Action – 2.2.4

   - 2.4 Self-Assessment Strategies – 2.4.2, 2.4.3, 2.4.4

3. Share knowledge and participate ethically and productively as members of our democratic society

   - 3.2 Dispositions in Action – 3.2.3

   - 3.4 Self-Assessment Strategies – 3.4.1, 3.4.3

Modifications for Special Education Students:

1. Station 1 - Remove the chart

2. Station 3 - Help students find the videos on the side after the initial video.

3. Station 4 - Remove Introduction and Slide 5. Work with students on understanding between what they see in the slide, the information in the pamphlet, and the purpose of protists.

Station 1 – Animal and Plant Cells

Method of Research: Using iDevices and manipulating the iCell educational app for information

Highest Bloom's Taxonomy Level: Analyzing

Directions: With a partner, use the iPad and the iPod touches to explore plant and animal cells.

- Open the iCell app.
- Select the Animal and the Plant pictures to see the cells.
- Move the cells around and click onto the parts to learn more about them.
- Work with your partner and the iCell app to determine similarities and differences between animal and plant cells.

Information to Research:

1. What are some similarities between the plant and animal cells -

2. What are some differences between the plant and animal cells -

Directions: Working with the same partner, use the word bank below to type the parts of a cell into the appropriate column of the chart. Each term can only be used in one column.

Information to Research:

Cell Membrane
Cell Wall
Centrioles
Chloroplast

Cytoplasm
Endoplasmic Reticulum
Golgi Body
Lysosomes

Mitochondrion
Nucleolus
Nucleus
Vacuole

Animal Cells ONLY	Plant Cells ONLY	BOTH Plant & Animal Cells

1. **THINKING QUESTION:** From what you can see, what are some things that make animal and plant cells different from one another?

Station 2 – Bacteria

Method of Research: Using subscription databases for information

Highest Bloom's Taxonomy Level: Applying

Directions: Independently, use the school subscription databases to research information on bacteria.

Information to Research:

1. What is bacteria?

2. What does bacteria do?

3. What are some diseases that bacteria cause?

4. Make a list of the pros (positives) and cons (negatives) of bacteria.

Pros	Cons

5. **THINKING QUESTION:** Is bacteria good or bad for people?

Station 3 – Fungi

Method of Research: Using a subscription video streaming service for information

Highest Bloom's Taxonomy Level: Understanding

> **Directions:** Independently, use Discovery Education videos to answer the questions below.
> - Go to Discovery Education: http://www.discoveryeducation.com
> - Login with your username and password
> - Search for the video "Welcome to the Wonderful World of Fungi" (1:03)
> - Watch the video and answer the questions. You may pause as you go, to answer questions.

Information to Research:

1. Why is fungi classified into its own biological kingdom?

2. Fungi are decomposers. What does this mean that fungi do?

> **Directions:** Use the videos to the right of "Welcome to the Wonderful World of Fungi" to answer the questions below. The videos to watch on the right are "Characteristics of Fungi," "Obtaining Food," and "Reproduction in Fungi."

Information to Research:

3. What are four characteristics of fungi?

4. How do fungi obtain food?

5. How do fungi reproduce?

6. **THINKING QUESTION:** Explain the important purpose fungi serve.

Station 4 – Protists

Method of Research: Using microviewers and text pamphlets for information

Highest Bloom's Taxonomy Level: Applying

Information to Research:

INTRODUCTION:

1. All protists have an organized _____.

2. In addition, all protists are single- _____ and live associated with _____.

SLIDE 1: AMOEBA (220X) Phylum Sarcodina

All members of this phylum resemble the amoeba because they have no_____.

SLIDE 2: PARAMECIUM (100x) Phylum Ciliophora

1. What type of protist is a paramecium?

2. What is the purpose of the **oral groove**?

SLIDE 5: EUGLENA (400X) Phylum Euglenapyta

1. Euglena have both characteristics of _____ and _____.

2. What helps the euglena make food?

Station 5 – Viruses

Method of Research: Watching a National Geographic Video for information

Highest Bloom's Taxonomy Level: Creating

Information to Research:

1. How long can it take for serious symptoms of the flu to occur?

2. How many flu pandemics have killed millions in the last century?

3. How was the flu of 1918 transmitted?

4. How many died from the flu virus of 1918?

5. How does a flu virus attack?

6. How does the human immune system react to a flu virus?

7. What can inflammation in the lungs cause in a patient with a severe form of the flu?

8. Flu viruses are made up of _____. What happens when the virus mutates?

9. Once human-to-human contact occurs for a new virus strain of the flu, what can happen?

10. **THINKING QUESTION:** What do you think people can do to make sure they don't spread the flu or other illnesses?

11. **THINKING QUESTION:** How would you generate a plan for the airlines to prevent illnesses from spreading?

Materials Needed for Cells Learning Stations

Station 1 – Plant and Animal Cells – iDevices and Educational App

- iPods / iPads/ iPhones

- iCell app from Apple Store

Station 2 – Bacteria – Databases

- School subscription databases: Bacteria

Station 3 – Fungi – Discovery Education Videos

- Discovery Education Videos
  - "Welcome to the Wonderful World of Fungi"
  - "Characteristics of Fungi"
  - "Obtaining Food"
  - "Reproduction in Fungi"
- Headphones
- Headphones sign

Station 4 – Protists – Microviewers and Pamphlets

- Materials from Life Science Teacher (McComas, William F. *Microviewer Lesson Set 22: "The Kingdom Protista."* Chippewa Falls: National Teaching Aids, 2001. Print.)
  - Microviewers
  - Slides for Microviewers
  - Pamphlets of information for the slides

Station 5 – Viruses – Video

- National Geographic Video: "How Flu Viruses Attack" - http://tinyurl.com/natgeofluvirus (original: http://video.nationalgeographic.com/video/news/history-archaeology-news/swine-flu-overview-vin/)
- Headphones
- Headphones sign

Rotation Song Suggestion: "Animal Cells" by Mr. Duey on Class Dis-missed CD

Student Pre-Self-Assessment:

These questions are to be answered before the lesson takes place. The questions can be multiple choice for data collection purposes or students may fill in the blank.

1. What are some differences between plant and animal cells? (If you haven't learned this yet or you don't know, put IDK.)
2. Is bacteria good or bad for humans? (If you haven't learned this yet or you don't know, put IDK.)
3. What does fungi do? (If you haven't learned this yet or you don't know, put IDK.)
4. What is a protist? (If you haven't learned this yet or you don't know, put IDK.)
5. Are viruses good or bad for humans? (If you haven't learned this yet or you don't know, put IDK.)
6. What is a good resource to use to find research? (If you haven't learned this yet or you don't know, put IDK.)

Student Post-Self-Assessment:

These questions are to be answered after the lesson takes place. Any or all of the following questions can be used in an assessment of your choice (see Chapter 6) for this set of multimedia learning stations. The questions can be multiple choice for data collection purposes or students may fill in the blank.

1. What are some differences between plant and animal cells?
2. Is bacteria good or bad for humans?
3. What does fungi do?
4. What is a protist?
5. Are viruses good or bad for humans?
6. What is a good resource to find research?

7. What learning stations did you find to be the most interesting? Check all that apply.

   - Station 1 - Plant and Animals Cells - iPads and iCell App

   - Station 2 - Bacteria - OneSearch

   - Station 3 - Fungi - Discovery Education Video

   - Station 4 - Protists - Microviewers and Pamphlets

   - Station 5 - Viruses - National Geographic Video

8. What would you change about your learning process if you were to do these stations again?

9. Overall, how would you assess your learning today?

   - I did extremely well. I learned a lot about my topic and would like to learn about more. I learned some research skills to use in the future.

   - I did well. I learned something about my topic and learned some tips on how to research that I can use in the future.

   - I did OK. I could have worked a little harder, but I learned something about my topic and researching.

   - I wasn't on my game today. I didn't learn nearly as much as I could have.

   - I didn't do anything today, so I didn't learn anything.

10. Kindly list any suggestions you have for improving these stations.

Big Project Assessment Option:

Create an informational poster on Glogster (http://edu.glogster.com/) that has information on each of the five organisms you researched today. The information should come from the research you gathered today during the multimedia learning stations.

Science 3

Rocks and Minerals Learning Stations

Created in collaboration with Shannon M. Smith

Grade Level: Earth Science (8–10)

Subject Standards from Virginia Standards of Learning

Science: http://www.doe.virginia.gov/testing/sol/standards_docs/science/index.shtml

Earth Science: ES.4, ES.5

AASL Standards

1. Inquire, think critically, and gain knowledge
   - 1.1 Skills – 1.1.1, 1.1.2, 1.1.3, 1.1.4, 1.1.5, 1.1.6, 1.1.7, 1.1.8, 1.1.9
   - 1.2 Dispositions in Action – 1.2.1, 1.2.2, 1.2.3, 1.2.4, 1.2.5, 1.2.6, 1.2.7
   - 1.3 Responsibilities – 1.3.1, 1.3.3, 1.3.5
   - 1.4 Self-Assessment Strategies – 1.4.1, 1.4.2, 1.4.3, 1.4.4

2. Draw conclusions, make informed decisions, apply knowledge to new situations, and create new knowledge.
   - 2.1 Skills – 2.1.1, 2.1.3, 2.1.4, 2.1.5, 2.1.6
   - 2.2 Dispositions in Action – 2.2.1, 2.2.4
   - 2.3 Responsibilities – 2.3.1, 2.3.2
   - 2.4 Self-Assessment Strategies – 2.4.1, 2.4.2, 2.4.3

3. Share knowledge and participate ethically and productively as members of our democratic society.
   - 3.1 Skills – 3.1.1, 3.1.5, 3.1.6
   - 3.2 Dispositions in Action – 3.2.1, 3.2.2, 3.2.3
   - 3.3 Responsibilities – 3.3.1
   - 3.4 Self-Assessment Strategies – 3.4.1, 3.4.2, 3.4.3

4. Pursue personal and aesthetic growth
   - 4.2 Dispositions in Action – 4.2.1
   - 4.3 Responsibilities – 4.3.2
   - 4.4 Self-assessment Strategies – 4.4.1

Note to Librarian:

1. Students should pick four of the nine stations in this set of multimedia learning stations to explore. They choose which four interest them the most.

2. Students may choose to work together or independently at one or more stations.

Modifications for Special Education Students:

Students should choose three stations to complete instead of four, or these stations can be spread over more than one 90-minute class period. The librarian and teacher should be readily available for assistance.

Station 1 – Diamonds OR Rock Cycle

Method of Research: Searching and reading educational apps for information

Highest Bloom's Taxonomy Level: Remembering

> **Directions:**
> - Use the apps under Rocks and Minerals on the iPad and/or two iPod Touches for this station.
> - Choose either "The Rock Cycle" or the "GIA 4C's Guide" app. Do not repeat a rock cycle or diamond station.
> - Set the timer and spend ten minutes "playing" with the apps to learn about as much as you can.

Information to Research:

What did you learn? Be *loquacious* in discussing the apps with any partners you have and in your written answer! You need to amaze me with the *breadth* of your new knowledge!

Station 2 – Mineral Makeup

Method of Research: Searching for and reading websites for information

Highest Bloom's Taxonomy Level: Evaluating

> **Directions:**
> Mineral makeup is very popular in cosmetic companies right now. Research what it is, how it is made, and what the benefits and/or disadvantages in using it are. You may use the websites below to help, or you may use other resources of your own. Remember to evaluate all websites to look for "actual - factual" information. You may use the web evaluation checklist provided to help guide you.
> - The Power of Minerals - http://tinyurl.com/minmakeup1 - Select "Learn More"
> - The Lowdown on Mineral Makeup - http://tinyurl.com/minmakeup2
> - Mineral Makeup Ingredients - The Ponte Vedra Soap Shoppe, Inc. - http://tinyurl.com/minmakeup3

Information to Research:

1. What is mineral makeup?
2. What minerals are found in mineral makeup?
3. Why are these minerals supposed to be good for the skin?
4. What are some possible drawbacks in using mineral makeup?
5. In your opinion, is mineral makeup better, the same, or not as good as regular cosmetics? Support your answer with evidence from your reading and research.
6. Use EasyBib (www.easybib.com) to cite the articles you used to support your theory in #5. Post your citations in MLA format below.

Works Cited:

Station 3 – Farming

Method of Research: Choosing website sources, evaluating and reading them for information

Highest Bloom's Taxonomy Level: Evaluating

Example Question: When are rocks beneficial in farming?

Good Search Terms: "rocks benefits farming"

Bad Search: "When are rocks beneficial in farming?" (We don't want to search for the words "why," "are," or "in")

Information to Research:

1. How are minerals used in farming?

2. What is the danger of mineral depletion in soil used for farming, and what do farmers do to try to combat this?

3. What challenges do farmers face with the rocks in the soil?

4. What are rock fertilizers, and how are they beneficial for farming?

5. Use EasyBib www.easybib.com to cite the sources you used for this research below.

Works Cited:

Station 4 – Careers

Method of Research: Choosing website sources, evaluating and reading them for information

Highest Bloom's Taxonomy Level: Evaluating

Example Question: What rocks and minerals do geologists use?

Good Search Terms: "geologist rocks" *or* "minerals use"

Bad Search: "What rocks and minerals do geologists use?" (We don't want to search for the words "what," "and," and "do")

Career List:

Civil Engineer
Construction worker
Cosmetic Maker
Dentist
Dietician
Doctor
Farmer (agricultural manager)
Gemologist

Geologist
Geotechnical Engineer
Jeweler
Miner
Mineralogist
Petrologist
Student Choice - Approve profession with teacher or librarian

Information to Research:

1. What does this career entail?

2. How are rocks and/or minerals important in this field?

3. What are some of the rocks and or minerals used in this job and how are they used?

4. How is this career important to society? How does it improve life, or how is it necessary or important for our lives?

5. What is an average salary for a worker in this field?

6. What kind of education is required for a person in this profession?

7. Why did this career interest you the most?

8. Use EasyBib www.easybib.com to cite the sources you used for this research below.

Works Cited:

Station 5 – Interactive Rock Cycle Website

Method of Research: Using an interactive website to gather and apply information

Highest Bloom's Taxonomy Level: Applying

Directions:
- Use the following website to learn more about rocks and the rock cycle http://tinyurl.com/rockcyclestation
- Keep selecting next to navigate through the pages
- Watch the animations to help with your understanding of rocks.

Information to Research:

1. What are igneous, sedimentary, and metamorphic rocks?

   - Igneous -

   - Sedimentary -

   - Metamorphic -

2. Create a virtual rock collection and show your teacher or librarian the completed collection.

3. Take the quiz, and show your teacher or librarian your final score.

4. What are some ways that rocks change?

5. How do rocks change into other types of rocks?

6. Do "Transform the Rock" and show your teacher or librarian your final product.

7. Do the "Rock Cycle Diagram" and show your teacher or librarian your final product.

8. Take the Assessment. What did you get?

Station 6 – A Diamond's Journey

Method of Research: Reading a website for information

Highest Bloom's Taxonomy Level: Analyzing

Directions:
- Watch MSNBC's video "A Diamond's Journey" to learn more about how a diamond gets from a mine to a jewelry store: http://tinyurl.com/diamondjourney
- Watch the Intro first. Use headphones.
- Then look at all the pictures for each stop in a diamond's journey.
- Select "Next" after each series of pictures is complete.

Information to Research:

1. Describe a diamond's journey. What is the process it goes through before it gets to a jewelry store?

2. Describe some of the lives of the people involved in a diamond's journey.

3. What were some of the expectations you had about diamond mining and what were some of the surprises?

4. What explanation do you have for why diamonds are expensive?

Station 7 – Prices of Precious Metals

Method of Research: Reading a website with charts for information

Highest Bloom's Taxonomy Level: Evaluating

Directions: Use the following website to determine the current prices for gold, silver, platinum, and copper: http://money.cnn.com/data/commodities

	$/troy ounce	Lowest cost in last 52-week period	Highest cost in last 52-week period	Has the price gone up or down in the last day
Gold	$	$	$	
Silver	$	$	$	
Platinum	$	$	$	
Copper	$	$	$	

Information to Research:

1. How many grams are in a troy ounce? (**Hint:** Google is very good at conversions. Type "convert troy ounces to grams" in the search box to get your answer.)

2. Which metal is in highest demand?

3. Do you think the metal that is usually in the highest demand is *always* in highest demand? Explain your rationale and be detailed in your answer!

4. Use the electronic balance at your table to measure the mass of the various objects on the table. These balances measure in grams. Which item is closest to one troy ounce?

5. Now that you see how much an ounce is, would you spend that much on the following metals? Gold? Silver? Platinum? Copper? Why or why not?

6. What could you use these metals for?

Station 8 – Natural Rock Formations

Method of Research: Searching for websites through images then reading them for information

Highest Bloom's Taxonomy Level: Understanding

Directions: Do a Google Image Search for natural rock formations in the United States. Look at some of the images and select a few that interest you. Evaluate the website where you found the image. If it is reliable, research the rock formation.

Make sure you create a citation in EasyBib (www.easybib.com) for each website used, so we can check your sources!

Name of the Rock Formation	Where it is found?	What type of rock is it?	How was it formed?

Works Cited:

Station 9 – Design Your Own Research

Method of Research: Selecting topic, questions and resources for information

Highest Bloom's Taxonomy Level: Creating

Design your own inquiry-based research topic.

Topic Ideas:

Questions:

Source Ideas:

Product (the method you will use to show me what you learned):

Works Cited:

Materials Needed for Rocks and Minerals Learning Stations

Station 1 – Diamonds OR Rock Cycle – Educational Apps

- iPad(s)
- iPod Touch(es)
- Chargers
- Apps "GIA 4C's Guide" and "The Rock Cycle"
- Stands for devices
- Headphones

Station 2 – Mineral Makeup – Websites

- Bare Escentuals Website: http://tinyurl.com/minmakeup1 (original: http://www.bareescentuals.com/on/demandware.store/Sites-BareEscentuals-Site/default/Experience-Show?cgid=BM_SUB_COMPLEXION)
- Web MD Healthy Beauty Information Website: http://tinyurl.com/minmakeup2 (original: http://www.webmd.com/healthy-beauty/features/the-lowdown-on-mineral-makeup)
- The Ponte Vedra Soap Shoppe, Inc. Website: http://tinyurl.com/minmakeup3 (original: http://www.pvsoap.com/mineral_makeup_ingredients.asp)
- School subscription databases
- Discovery Education

- Sweet Search, Google, Bing

- Web Evaluation Form

- EasyBib Website: http:www.easybib.com

Station 3 – Farming – Choice of Resources

- School subscription databases

- Discovery Education

- Sweet Search, Google, Bing

- Web Evaluation Form

- EasyBib Website: http:www.easybib.com

Station 4 – Careers – Choice of Resources

- School subscription databases

- Discovery Education

- Sweet Search, Google, Bing

- Web Evaluation Form

- EasyBib Website: http:www.easybib.com

Station 5 – Interactive Rock Cycle – Website

- Annenberg Learner: Interactives: Rock Cycle Website: http://tinyurl.com/rockcyclestation (original: http://www.learner.org/interactives/rockcycle/index.html)

- Snipping Tool

Station 6 –A Diamond's Journey – Website

- MSNBC Website: A Diamond's Journey: http://tinyurl.com/diamondjourney (original: http://www.msnbc.msn.com/id/15842546/0)

- Headphones

Station 7 – Prices of Precious Metals – Website

- CNN Website - Money: http://money.cnn.com/data/commodities/

- Google

- Electronic balance

- Items to measure for mass

Station 8 – Natural Rock Formations – Google Images & Websites

- Google Images
- Web Evaluation Form
- EasyBib Website: http:www.easybib.com

Station 9 – Design Your Own Research – Choice of Resources

- School subscription databases
- Discovery Education
- Sweet Search, Google, Bing
- Web Evaluation Form
- EasyBib Website: http:www.easybib.com

Rotation Song Suggestion (if rotations are timed): "3 Rocks" by Mr. Duey on *Class Dis-missed* CD

Student Pre-Self-Assessment:

These questions are to be answered before the lesson takes place. The questions can be multiple choice for data collection purposes or students may fill in the blank.

1. What is a good source to use for science research? (If you haven't learned this before or you don't know, put IDK.)
2. What are some uses for rocks? (If you haven't learned this before or you don't know, put IDK.)
3. What are some uses for minerals? (If you haven't learned this before or you don't know, put IDK.)

Student Post-Self-Assessment:

These questions are to be answered after the lesson takes place. Any or all of the following questions can be used in an assessment of your choice (see Chapter 6) for this set of multimedia learning stations. The questions can be multiple choice for data collection purposes or students may fill in the blank.

1. What is a good source to use for research?
2. What are some uses for rocks?
3. What are some uses for minerals?
4. What is something specific you learned today that surprised you?
5. Complete this sentence. "After today, when I research, I am still struggling with . . ."
6. What learning stations did you find to be the most interesting? Check all that apply:
   - Station 1 - Diamonds OR Rock Cycle - Educational Apps
   - Station 2 - Mineral Makeup - Websites
   - Station 3 - Farming - Choice of Resources
   - Station 4 - Careers - Choice of Resources
   - Station 5 - Interactive Rock Cycle - Website

Who?	Yes	No
Is the author or the organization of the website listed?	☐	☐
Is a biography with the author's qualifications or information about the organization included?	☐	☐
Is contact information for the author or organization available?	☐	☐
Is the website sponsored by an educational (.edu) or governmental (.gov) organization?	☐	☐

What?	Yes	No
Is the purpose of the website stated or obvious?	☐	☐
Does the website state only facts, not opinions?	☐	☐
Do you think the images on this website are helpful, accurate, and real?	☐	☐
Is the information stated on this website the same as other websites?	☐	☐
Does the title of the website tell you what it is about?	☐	☐
Do you think the information on the website is real and true?	☐	☐

When?	Yes	No
Does the website have a date listed for when it was published or last updated?	☐	☐
Has the website been updated within the past year?	☐	☐
Are the links on the website active (do they work)?	☐	☐

Where?	Yes	No
Are you able to determine where the author or organization found the information for the website?	☐	☐
Did the author or organization create a works cited list, a bibliography, or a reference list?	☐	☐

Why?	Yes	No
Is this information useful for your purpose?	☐	☐

How?	Yes	No
Is the website free of spelling errors and grammatical mistakes?	☐	☐
Is the website organized in a logical order?	☐	☐
Is the website free of advertisements?	☐	☐
Is the website free of words such as "always," "never," "best," or "worst?"	☐	☐

Final Evaluation?	Yes	No
Do you think the publishing author or organization is an expert about the content on the website?	☐	☐
Do you trust that the information on this website is reliable?	☐	☐
will you use this website?	☐	☐

Created by Jen Spisak and Danielle Sommers
With revision assistance from Lynsie Levay, Kristy Eshmont, and Lisa Scott

Web Evaluation Checklist

- Station 6 - A Diamond's Journey - Website
- Station 7 - Prices of Precious Metals - Website
- Station 8 - Natural Rock Formations - Google Images & Websites
- Station 9 - Design Your Own Research - Choice of Resources

7. What would you change about your learning process if you were to do these stations again?

8. Overall, how would you assess your learning today?

- I did extremely well. I learned a lot about my topic and wonder about more. I learned some research skills to use in the future.

- I did well. I learned something about my topic and how to research in the future.

- I did OK. I could have worked a little harder, but I learned something about my topic and researching.

- I wasn't on my game today. I didn't learn nearly as much as I could have.

- I didn't do anything today, so I didn't learn anything.

9. Kindly list any suggestions you have for improving these stations.

Big Project Assessment Option:

Instead of offering "Station 9 - Design Your Own Research" as one of the choices students have during their multimedia learning stations, this can be expanded upon after class as a larger research project.

References

Access the Next Generation Science Standards by Topic. (2014). Retrieved December 14, 2014, from http://standards.nsta.org/AccessStandardsByTopic.aspx

Anderson, L. W., & Krathwohl, D. R. (2001). *A taxonomy for learning, teaching, and assessing: A revision of Bloom's taxonomy of educational objectives*. New York: Longman.

Bloom, B. S. (1956). *Taxonomy of educational objectives; The classification of educational goals*. New York: Longmans, Green.

Doeden, M., Barnett, C., & Hoover, D. (2005). *Boston Tea Party*. Mankato, MN: Capstone Press.

Dunn, R. (2001). Learning Style Differences of Nonconforming Middle-School Students. *NASSP Bulletin, 85*(626), 68–74. Retrieved from http://www.sagepub.com/eis2study/articles/Dunn.pdf

Dunn, R., & Dunn, K. (1978). *Teaching students through their individual learning styles: A practical approach*. Reston, VA: Reston Publishing Company.

Fluckiger, J. (2010). Single Point Rubric: A Tool for Responsible Student Self-Assessment. *Delta Kappa Gamma Bulletin, 76*(4), 18–25. Retrieved March 8, 2012, from https://www.dkg.org/sites/default/files/files-for-download/bulletin_vol76-4_2010summer.pdf

Formative vs Summative Assessment. (n.d.). Retrieved August 31, 2014, from http://www.cmu.edu/teaching/assessment/basics/formative-summative.html

Gardner, H. (1983). *Frames of mind: The theory of multiple intelligences*. New York: Basic Books.

Gonzalez, J. (2014, October 9). Your Rubric Is a Hot Mess; Here's How to Fix It. Brilliant or Insane Web site. Retrieved November 17, 2014, from http://www.brilliant-insane.com/2014/10/single-point-rubric.html

Harada, V. H., & Yoshina, J. M. (2010). *Assessing for Learning: Librarians and Teachers as Partners*. Santa Barbara, CA: Libraries Unlimited.

Israel, E. (2002). Examining Multiple Perspectives in Literature. In J. Holden & J. S. Schmidt (Eds.), *Inquiry and the literary text: Constructing discussions in the English classroom*. Urbana, IL: National Council of Teachers of English.

Jensen, E. (2005). Movement and Learning. In *Teaching with the brain in mind* (pp. 29–40). Alexandria, VA: Association for Supervision and Curriculum Development.

Marzano, R. J., & Kendall, J. S. (2007). *The new taxonomy of educational objectives*. Thousand Oaks, CA: Corwin Press.

Ravitch, D. (2007). *Edspeak: A glossary of education terms, phrases, buzzwords, and jargon* (p. 75). Alexandria, VA: Association for Supervision and Curriculum Development.

Rothstein, D., & Santana, L. (2011). *Make just one change: Teach students to ask their own questions.* Cambridge, MA: Harvard Education Press.

Schrock, K. (2011). Bloomin' Apps. Retrieved November 16, 2014, from http://www.schrockguide .net/bloomin-apps.html

Standards of Learning (SOL) & Testing. (2012). Retrieved December 14, 2014, from http://www.doe .virginia.gov/testing/index.shtml

Standards for the 21st-century learner in action. (2009). Chicago, IL: American Association of School Librarians.

Tomlinson, C. (1999). Mapping a route toward differentiated instruction. *Educational Leadership, 57*(1), 12–16.

Tomlinson, C. (2013). Differentiating instruction is . . . Retrieved November 15, 2014, from http:// www.caroltomlinson.com/

Walsh, J. A., & Sattes, B. D. (2008). *Quilt teacher manual* (2nd ed.). Charleston, WV: Edvantia.

Zmuda, A. (2010). *Breaking free from myths about teaching and learning: Innovation as an engine for student success.* Alexandria, VA: ASCD.

Index

About the Author

JEN SPISAK is a library information specialist at Hungary Creek Middle School in Henrico County, VA, who has published articles in Library Media Connection. Spisak received a master's degree in curriculum and instruction from Virginia Tech and completed her library course work at Virginia Commonwealth University. In 2012, the Virginia Association of School Librarians named her the Virginia School Librarian of the Year.